I0016999

Chapter 0 - Introduction

Chapter 0.1 - Why SQL is an important skill for software developers

In today's data-driven world, it is essential for software developers to possess SQL skills. SQL (Structured Query Language) is a standard programming language for managing and manipulating data stored in relational databases. It is an integral part of database management systems (DBMS) such as Microsoft SQL Server, MySQL, Oracle, and PostgreSQL.

Software developers use SQL to design, create, modify, and manage databases, which are the backbone of many software applications. In this chapter, we will discuss why SQL is an important skill for software developers to have and how it can benefit them in their careers.

SQL is a ubiquitous language in the industry

SQL is one of the most widely used programming languages in the industry, and it is used by developers, data analysts, data scientists, and database administrators. It is a language that is well-understood and supported by virtually all relational databases as well as data analytics tools. As a result, learning SQL can provide you with a strong foundation for working with databases and data in general across different platforms and environments.

SQL is essential for working with databases

Databases are the backbone of most software applications, and SQL is the language used to interact with them. As a software developer, you need to understand SQL to be able to perform tasks such as creating tables, inserting data, retrieving data, updating data, and deleting data from a database.

Being proficient in SQL can help you write more efficient and effective code by allowing you to optimise queries and reduce database load. It can also help you better understand the underlying structure of databases and how data is organised, which can inform your design decisions.

As a software developer, we spend a lot of our time debugging issues with our code, and being a skilled user of SQL can vastly improve the speed and efficiency with which you debug a problem. By being able to directly look at the data behind an issue, you can often get to the heart of a problem, since if the data is wrong then no matter of changing the code will solve that problem, you are better to resolve the issue at the source.

SQL is used for data analysis and reporting

SQL is a powerful tool for data analysis and reporting. With SQL, you can extract and manipulate large amounts of data from databases quickly and easily. You can also use SQL to perform complex calculations and generate reports that can be used to inform business decisions.

As a software developer, having the ability to perform data analysis and reporting can be a valuable skill. It can help you better understand the needs of your customers and stakeholders and make informed decisions about product development.

SQL is a transferable skill

SQL is a transferable skill that can be used across different industries and job roles. It is used in a wide range of fields, including finance, healthcare, education, and government. If you have SQL skills, you can apply them to different projects and roles, giving you more career flexibility and opportunities.

SQL is constantly evolving

SQL is constantly evolving, with new features and capabilities being added all the time. As a software developer, it is important to stay up-to-date with the latest advancements in SQL to ensure that you are using the language to its full potential.

For example, Microsoft SQL Server 2019 introduced new features such as Big Data Clusters and Machine Learning Services that allow developers to analyze and process large amounts of data using SQL. By keeping up with these advancements, you can stay ahead of the curve and provide more value to your clients and employers.

SQL is in high demand

SQL skills are in high demand in the job market. According to the 2020 Stack Overflow Developer Survey, SQL is the second most popular language among developers, after JavaScript. The survey also found that 47.5% of developers use SQL as part of their daily work.

Having SQL skills on your resume can make you a more attractive candidate for software development jobs, especially those that require database management and data analysis.

SQL can improve your problem-solving skills

SQL requires a logical and methodical approach to solving problems. To be proficient in SQL, you need to be able to break down complex problems into smaller, more manageable components and then develop a step-by-step plan to solve them.

These problem-solving skills are transferable to other areas of software development and can help you become a better problem solver in general. Additionally, SQL can help you develop a better understanding of how data is organised and how it can be manipulated, which can improve your ability to develop more efficient and effective software solutions.SQL can help you work more efficiently

As a software developer, your time is valuable. SQL can help you work more efficiently by allowing you to automate repetitive tasks, such as data entry and manipulation. This can save you time and help you focus on more complex and creative aspects of software development.

Additionally, SQL can help you avoid errors and ensure data integrity. By using SQL to manage and manipulate data, you can reduce the risk of errors caused by manual data entry and manipulation. This can help you deliver higher quality software solutions that meet your clients' needs.

SQL can help you communicate with non-technical stakeholders

SQL can help you communicate with non-technical stakeholders, such as business owners and managers. By using SQL to perform data analysis and reporting, you can generate reports and visualisations that are easy to understand and can help stakeholders make informed decisions.

Additionally, SQL can help you explain technical concepts to non-technical stakeholders by providing a way to demonstrate how data is organised and manipulated. This can help you build trust and credibility with your clients and stakeholders, which can lead to more business opportunities and partnerships.

SQL can help you become a better software developer

SQL can help you become a better software developer by providing you with a deeper understanding of databases and data management. This understanding can inform your design decisions and help you develop more efficient and effective software solutions.

Additionally, SQL can help you develop better coding habits by encouraging you to write more structured and efficient code. By optimising your SQL queries and reducing database load, you can create software solutions that are faster, more reliable, and easier to maintain.

Conclusion

SQL is an important skill for software developers to have. It is a ubiquitous language in the industry, essential for working with databases, used for data analysis and reporting, transferable across different industries and job roles, constantly evolving, in high demand, can improve your problem-solving skills, can help you work more efficiently, can help you communicate with non-technical stakeholders, and can help you become a better software developer.

Learning SQL can open up new career opportunities and provide you with a deeper understanding of data management and analysis. It can also help you become a more efficient and effective software developer, providing you with the tools and skills you need to deliver high-quality software solutions that meet your clients' needs.

If you are a software developer looking to expand your skills, learning SQL can be a great investment in your future. By mastering SQL, you can become a more well-rounded developer and increase your value to potential employers.

There are many resources available to help you learn SQL, including online courses, tutorials, and books. Many of these resources are free or low-cost, making it easy to get started with SQL even if you are on a tight budget.

When learning SQL, it is important to focus on practical applications and real-world scenarios. While it is important to understand the underlying principles of SQL, the best way to learn is by practising with real data and real-world scenarios. By working with real data, you can develop your problem-solving skills and gain practical experience that will be valuable in your career.

If you are already familiar with SQL, it is important to stay up-to-date with the latest trends and advancements in the field. SQL is constantly evolving, with new features and capabilities being added all the time. By staying up-to-date with the latest developments, you can ensure that your skills remain relevant and valuable in the industry.

Finally, SQL is an essential skill for software developers in today's data-driven world. By mastering SQL, you can become a more well-rounded and valuable developer, able to work with databases, analyse data, and communicate with non-technical stakeholders. Whether you are just starting out in your career or are a seasoned developer looking to expand your skill set, learning SQL can be a great investment in your future.

Chapter 0.2 - About the Author

Jim Brown is an innovative Head of Software Development with over 12 years of experience working in all aspects of the software development process. From concept to delivery of high-quality bespoke technology, Jim has consistently demonstrated his technical expertise and leadership skills in managing successful projects.

As a motivated technical team leader, Jim is skilled in advanced development methodologies, software development tools, and processes, contributing to highly efficient and well-tested project development. He is known for his excellent troubleshooting skills, able to quickly identify the root cause of problems and develop robust and efficient solutions within tight deadlines.

Currently serving as the Head of Software Development at a leading UK travel agency, Jim leads a growing team of highly skilled developers, delivering high-quality products within challenging timelines. He has extensive experience in leading complex projects and managing stakeholders across various departments. In his role, Jim directly manages three Scrum teams, working on developing new technology and supporting existing tech across all areas of the organisation, including the frontend website, sales-facing CRM, backend CMS, and other critical systems. He also acts as the systems architect for all new projects presented to the IT department and oversees non-technical aspects of the IT team, including QA, BA, and design teams.

Jim holds a BSc in Computer Science from the University of Worcester and has pursued continuous professional development through certifications such as Microsoft SQL Server 2012 for DBAs and Akamai Web Performance Certified Administrator. He is also an ILM Level 3 Leadership and Management certified professional.

Beyond his professional pursuits, Jim actively seeks to expand his knowledge and skills. He has been involved in various projects, including iOS development, where he worked on troubleshooting applications and location-based data requests and responses. Additionally, Jim has contributed to the technical development of a science fiction and entertainment blog, showcasing his expertise in WordPress customization and plugin development.

With his extensive experience, technical prowess, and leadership abilities, Jim Brown brings a wealth of knowledge and expertise to the field of software development and specifically where it comes to SQL and Database technology. This book serves as a testament to his commitment to excellence and his passion for delivering innovative and high-quality solutions.

Chapter 0.3 - Varieties of SQL

SQL (Structured Query Language) is a programming language used for managing and manipulating data in relational databases. SQL is a standard language, but there are many different varieties of SQL databases that exist. In this chapter, we will discuss some of the most popular SQL varieties used by software developers.

MySQL

MySQL is an open-source relational database management system (RDBMS) that is widely used by software developers. It was developed by MySQL AB, which was later acquired by Oracle Corporation. MySQL is written in C and C++ and is available for multiple platforms such as Windows, Linux, and macOS. MySQL is known for its scalability, ease of use, and robustness. Many web applications, including Facebook, Twitter, and YouTube, use MySQL as their primary database.

SQL Server

SQL Server is a relational database management system developed by Microsoft. It is one of the most popular databases used in enterprise environments. SQL Server is known for its scalability, high availability, and security features. SQL Server is available in various editions, including Express, Standard, and Enterprise, making it suitable for businesses of all sizes.

Oracle Database

Oracle Database is an object-relational database management system developed by Oracle Corporation. It is known for its robustness, high availability, and scalability. Oracle Database supports SQL, PL/SQL, and Java, making it a versatile database system. It is widely used in large enterprise environments, including financial services and government organisations.

PostgreSQL

PostgreSQL is an open-source object-relational database management system that is known for its robustness, scalability, and compliance with SQL standards. PostgreSQL supports a wide range of programming languages such as Python, Java, and C/C++. It is widely used in various applications, including web applications, scientific research, and financial services.

SQLite

SQLite is an open-source, lightweight, and self-contained relational database management system. It is widely used in embedded systems, mobile applications, and small-scale web applications. SQLite is known for its ease of use, portability, and high performance.

MongoDB

MongoDB is a NoSQL database management system that uses a document-oriented data model. It is widely used in web applications and other applications that require high scalability and flexibility. MongoDB is known for its high performance, scalability, and ease of use.

Conclusion

In this chapter, we have discussed some of the most popular SQL varieties used by software developers. Each of these SQL varieties has its own strengths and weaknesses, making them suitable for different types of applications. As a software developer, it is essential to choose the right database system based on the application's requirements and the project's goals.

Throughout the rest of this book, we will focus on SQL Server. If you would prefer to look at a different type of SQL, please see my other published works to find the specific version that suits you.

Chapter 1: Getting Started with SQL Server

Chapter 1.1 - Basic Concepts and Terminology of SQL

As a software developer, it is essential to have a good understanding of the basic concepts and terminology of SQL. In this chapter, we will cover some of the most important concepts and terms used in SQL.

Welcome to the world of Microsoft SQL Server, a powerful and versatile relational database management system designed to empower software developers in building robust, scalable, and efficient applications. In this chapter, we will embark on a journey to explore the fundamental concepts and terminology of SQL Server, laying the foundation for your mastery of this essential technology.

Understanding SQL Server:

At its core, SQL Server is a database platform developed by Microsoft, known for its comprehensive set of features, reliability, and performance. SQL Server allows you to store, manage, and manipulate vast amounts of data while offering a seamless integration with other Microsoft products and services.

SQL - The Language of SQL Server

Structured Query Language (SQL) is the primary language used to communicate with SQL Server. SQL provides a standardised way to interact with the database, enabling you to perform various operations, such as querying data, inserting new records, updating existing ones, and deleting information. Understanding SQL is crucial for harnessing the full potential of SQL Server.

Relational Databases

SQL Server falls under the category of Relational Database Management Systems (RDBMS).
A relational database is a collection of data that is organised into tables. Each table represents a logical grouping of related data, and each row in a table represents a single instance of that data. For example, a database for an online store might have tables for customers, orders, and products.

Relational databases serve as the backbone of modern data management systems, and understanding their fundamentals is crucial for software developers. A relational database organises and stores data in a structured manner, using tables composed of rows and columns. These tables establish relationships between entities, allowing for efficient data retrieval, manipulation, and analysis. Real-world applications abound in diverse industries: in e-commerce, a relational database facilitates the management of products, orders, and customers; in healthcare, it enables the storage and retrieval of patient records, diagnoses, and treatments; in finance, it supports transactions, account balances, and financial reporting. The versatility and power of relational databases make them an essential tool for software developers, enabling the construction of robust and scalable systems to handle complex data needs.

Tables

A table is a collection of related data organised into rows and columns. Each column in a table represents a specific piece of information, such as a customer's name or address, and each row represents a single instance of that information.

Tables are fundamental components of a relational database, serving as containers for organising and storing data in a structured manner. Each table consists of rows and columns, representing records and attributes, respectively. In a software development context, tables can be thought of as analogous to objects or entities in an application's data model. For example, in an e-commerce system, a "Products" table may contain columns such as "ProductID," "ProductName," "Price," and "Quantity," with each row representing a unique product entry. Tables define the schema of a database, specifying the names and data types of columns, as well as constraints, such as primary keys, foreign keys, and indexes. By structuring data into tables, developers can efficiently store, retrieve, and manipulate information, enabling seamless interactions with the underlying database system. Tables form the backbone of a relational database, providing a flexible and scalable framework for managing and organising data effectively.

Columns

A column, also known as a field, is a vertical element in a table that represents a specific type of data, such as a customer's name or address. Each column has a unique name and data type, which determines the type of data that can be stored in it.

Columns play a crucial role in defining the structure and characteristics of a relational database table. In essence, a column represents a specific attribute or property of the data stored within a table. It serves as a named container for a particular type of information, such as names, dates, numbers, or textual descriptions.

For instance, in an "Employees" table, columns might include "EmployeeID," "FirstName," "LastName," "Email," and "DateOfBirth." Each column is assigned a specific data type, which determines the kind of data that can be stored in it, ensuring data integrity and consistency. Columns can also have additional properties, such as constraints, defaults, and indexes, to further refine their behaviour and optimise data operations. By organising data into columns, software developers can efficiently store, retrieve, and manipulate specific attributes, allowing for flexible and granular data management within a relational database. Columns provide the building blocks for creating structured and meaningful representations of real-world entities and attributes in the digital realm.

Data Types

A data type is a classification of data based on its characteristics. SQL Server supports several data types, including integer, decimal, varchar, date, and time. Each data type has a specific range of values and requires a certain amount of storage space.

Data types are essential components in defining the nature and characteristics of data stored within a relational database table. They provide a way to categorise and restrict the kind of values that can be stored in a particular column. SQL Server offers a wide range of data types, including common ones like integers, decimals, strings, dates, and booleans, as well as more specialised types for handling spatial data, XML, or binary data.

Choosing the appropriate data type for each column is crucial for optimising storage, ensuring data accuracy, and improving performance. For example, using an integer data type for a column that only needs to store whole numbers will save storage space and allow for efficient mathematical calculations. Understanding the available data types and their characteristics empowers software developers to design robust database schemas and make informed decisions regarding data storage and manipulation. By leveraging the right data types, developers can ensure data integrity, enhance query efficiency, and enable effective data analysis and reporting within a relational database system.

Primary Key

A primary key is a unique identifier for each row in a table. It is used to ensure that each row in a table is unique and to establish relationships between tables. A primary key can be a single column or a combination of columns.

Foreign Key

A foreign key is a column in a table that refers to the primary key of another table. It is used to establish relationships between tables and ensure data integrity. A foreign key can be a single column or a combination of columns.

Constraints

Constraints are rules that are enforced on the data in a table. They are used to ensure data integrity and prevent invalid data from being inserted or updated. SQL Server supports several types of constraints, including NOT NULL, UNIQUE, PRIMARY KEY, and FOREIGN KEY.

Queries

A query is a request for data from one or more tables in a database. Queries are used to retrieve, insert, update, and delete data in a database. The most common type of query is the SELECT statement, which is used to retrieve data from one or more tables.

Queries are an integral part of working with relational databases, providing a powerful means to retrieve, manipulate, and analyse data. A query is a request for information from a database that follows a specific syntax and structure defined by the SQL (Structured Query Language) standard. With queries, software developers can express their data requirements and extract relevant data from one or more database tables. SQL Server offers a comprehensive set of query capabilities, allowing developers to perform a wide range of operations such as selecting specific columns, filtering rows based on conditions, sorting data, joining tables, aggregating data, and performing complex calculations. Queries can also incorporate conditions, subqueries, and functions to manipulate and transform data as needed. By mastering the art of querying, developers can harness the full potential of a relational database, enabling them to retrieve precise information, generate reports, perform data analysis, and build efficient and responsive applications.

SELECT Statement

The SELECT statement is used to retrieve data from one or more tables in a database. It allows you to specify the columns you want to retrieve and any filters or sorting you want to apply to the data. Here is an example of a basic SELECT statement:

```
SELECT * FROM Customers;
```

In this example, we are retrieving all of the data from the Customers table.

So far In this chapter, we have covered some of the basic concepts and terminology of SQL. We have learned about relational databases, tables, columns, data types, primary and foreign keys, constraints, and queries. These concepts are essential for software developers who need to work with SQL Server. In the next chapter, we will dive deeper into SQL Server and explore some more advanced concepts such as joins, subqueries, and stored procedures.

Now let us look at some more features of SQL server.

Subqueries

A subquery is a query that is nested within another query. It is used to retrieve data that will be used in another query or as a filter for a specific set of data. Subqueries can be used in various parts of a query, including the SELECT, FROM, and WHERE clauses.

Here is an example of a subquery used in the WHERE clause:

```
SELECT *
FROM Customers
WHERE CustomerID IN (SELECT CustomerID FROM Orders);
```

In this example, the subquery retrieves all CustomerIDs from the Orders table, and the outer query retrieves all rows from the Customers table where the CustomerID is in the list of CustomerIDs from the subquery.

Stored Procedures

A stored procedure is a precompiled set of SQL statements that can be executed on demand. It is similar to a function in other programming languages, but it is stored in the database and can be called from any application that has access to the database.

Stored procedures can be used to perform complex data operations, validate data, and enforce business rules. They can also be used to improve database performance by reducing network traffic and minimising the number of round trips to the database.

Here is an example of a simple stored procedure:

```sql
CREATE PROCEDURE GetCustomers
AS
BEGIN
  SELECT *
  FROM Customers;
END;
```

In this example, the stored procedure called GetCustomers retrieves all rows from the Customers table.

Now we have explored some of the more advanced concepts and features of SQL Server. We have learned about joins, subqueries, and stored procedures, which are essential tools for software developers working with SQL Server. These features allow developers to retrieve and manipulate data in more complex ways, and they can help improve database performance and data integrity. In the next chapter, we will cover some best practices for working with SQL Server and how to optimise your database for better performance.

Chapter 1.2 - Setting up a SQL Server Database and Creating Tables

SQL Server is a powerful and widely used database management system (DBMS) developed by Microsoft. It is used to store, retrieve, and manage data for a variety of applications. As a software developer, setting up a SQL Server database and creating tables is an essential skill to have. In this chapter, we will go through the process of setting up a SQL Server database and creating tables step-by-step.

Before we start, let's define some key terms that will be used throughout this chapter:

Database: A collection of data that is organised in a specific way and can be accessed and managed by a DBMS.
Table: A collection of related data organised in rows and columns.
Column: A vertical line in a table that defines a specific type of data.
Row: A horizontal line in a table that represents a record.
Primary key: A unique identifier for a row in a table.
Foreign key: A column in one table that refers to the primary key of another table.
Setting up SQL Server

The first step to setting up a SQL Server database is to install SQL Server on your computer. SQL Server can be downloaded from the Microsoft website, and there are different versions available depending on your needs. Once you have downloaded and installed SQL Server, you can start the SQL Server Management Studio (SSMS) application, which is used to manage SQL Server databases.

Creating a Database

To create a database in SQL Server, you can use the following steps:

Open SSMS and connect to your SQL Server instance.
In the Object Explorer pane, right-click on the Databases folder and select New Database.
In the New Database dialog box, enter a name for your database and click OK.
Once you have created your database, you can start creating tables to store your data.

Creating Tables

Tables are the building blocks of a SQL Server database. They are used to store data in a structured way, and they can be created using the following syntax:

```
CREATE TABLE table_name
(
    column1 datatype [NULL | NOT NULL],
    column2 datatype [NULL | NOT NULL],
    ...
    PRIMARY KEY (one or more columns)
    FOREIGN KEY (one or more columns) REFERENCES other_table (one or
more columns)
);
```

Let's break down this syntax:

CREATE TABLE: This is a SQL command that is used to create a new table.
table_name: This is the name of the table that you want to create.
column1, column2, ...: These are the names of the columns in the table.
datatype: This specifies the data type of the column. There are several data types available in SQL Server, such as int, varchar, and datetime.
NULL | NOT NULL: This specifies whether the column can contain null values or not.
PRIMARY KEY: This specifies the primary key for the table. The primary key is a unique identifier for each row in the table.
FOREIGN KEY: This specifies a column in the table that refers to the primary key of another table.
Let's create a sample table to demonstrate how to use this syntax:

```
CREATE TABLE Customers
(
    CustomerID int NOT NULL PRIMARY KEY,
    FirstName varchar(50) NOT NULL,
    LastName varchar(50) NOT NULL,
    Email varchar(50),
    Phone varchar(20),
    Address varchar(100),
    City varchar(50),
    State varchar(50),
    ZipCode varchar(10)
);
```

In this example, we have created a table called Customers with several columns, including a primary key column called CustomerID. The CustomerID column is of the int data type and is marked as NOT NULL, which means that it cannot contain null values. The FirstName and LastName columns are of the varchar data type and are also marked as NOT NULL. The

Email, Phone, Address, City, State, and ZipCode columns are all optional and can contain null values.

Now that we have created our table, we can start inserting data into it.

Inserting Data

To insert data into a SQL Server table, you can use the following syntax:

```sql
INSERT INTO table_name (column1, column2, ..., columnN)
VALUES (value1, value2, ..., valueN);
```

Let's insert some sample data into our Customers table:

```sql
INSERT INTO Customers (CustomerID, FirstName, LastName, Email, Phone,
Address, City, State, ZipCode)
VALUES (1, 'John', 'Doe', 'john.doe@email.com', '555-1234', '123 Main
St', 'Anytown', 'CA', '12345');

INSERT INTO Customers (CustomerID, FirstName, LastName, Email, Phone,
Address, City, State, ZipCode)
VALUES (2, 'Jane', 'Smith', 'jane.smith@email.com', '555-5678', '456
Park Ave', 'Anycity', 'NY', '67890');
```

In these examples, we have inserted two rows of data into the Customers table. Each row contains values for all of the columns in the table.

Querying Data

To retrieve data from a SQL Server table, you can use the SELECT statement. The SELECT statement is used to retrieve data from one or more tables, and it can be customized using several keywords and clauses.

Here is an example of a basic SELECT statement:

```sql
SELECT * FROM Customers;
```

In this example, we are retrieving all of the data from the Customers table. The * symbol is a wildcard that represents all of the columns in the table.

Here is another example that retrieves specific columns:

```sql
SELECT FirstName, LastName, Email FROM Customers;
```

In this example, we are retrieving only the FirstName, LastName, and Email columns from the Customers table.

Conclusion

In this chapter, we have covered the basics of setting up a SQL Server database and creating tables. We have learned how to create a database, how to create tables with columns and constraints, how to insert data into tables, and how to retrieve data using the SELECT statement. These skills are essential for software developers who need to manage data using SQL Server. In the next chapter, we will dive deeper into SQL Server and learn more advanced concepts such as joins, subqueries, and stored procedures.

Chapter 1.3 - Inserting, updating, and deleting data

In SQL Server, inserting, updating, and deleting data are essential operations for managing a database. These operations are performed using SQL statements, and can be executed using various tools such as SQL Server Management Studio or through programming languages such as C# or Java.

In this chapter, we will cover the basics of inserting, updating, and deleting data in SQL Server, and provide examples of how to use these operations in different scenarios.

Inserting Data

The INSERT statement is used to insert new rows into a table. The basic syntax of the INSERT statement is as follows:

```
INSERT INTO table_name (column1, column2, column3, ...)
VALUES (value1, value2, value3, ...);
```

In this syntax, table_name is the name of the table where you want to insert the data, and column1, column2, column3, etc. are the names of the columns where you want to insert the values.

The VALUES clause contains the actual values that you want to insert into the table. The values must match the data type of the columns in the table.

Let's take a look at an example:

```
INSERT INTO employees (first_name, last_name, email, phone)
VALUES ('John', 'Doe', 'john.doe@email.com', '555-555-5555');
```

In this example, we are inserting a new row into the employees table with the values 'John' for the first_name column, 'Doe' for the last_name column, 'john.doe@email.com' for the email column, and '555-555-5555' for the phone column.

If you want to insert data into all columns of a table, you can omit the column list in the INSERT statement. However, this is not recommended because it can cause errors if the order of the values does not match the order of the columns in the table.

```
INSERT INTO employees
VALUES ('Jane', 'Doe', 'jane.doe@email.com', '555-555-5555');
```

In this example, we are inserting a new row into the employees table without specifying the column names. The values are inserted in the order of the columns in the table.

Updating Data

The UPDATE statement is used to modify existing rows in a table. The basic syntax of the UPDATE statement is as follows:

```
UPDATE table_name
SET column1 = value1, column2 = value2, column3 = value3, ...
WHERE condition;
```

In this syntax, table_name is the name of the table where you want to update the data, and column1, column2, column3, etc. are the names of the columns that you want to update.

The SET clause contains the new values that you want to set for the columns. The values must match the data type of the columns in the table.

The WHERE clause specifies which rows you want to update. If you omit the WHERE clause, all rows in the table will be updated with the new values.

Let's take a look at an example:

```
UPDATE employees
SET phone = '555-555-1234'
WHERE last_name = 'Doe';
```

In this example, we are updating the phone column of all rows in the employees table where the last_name column is 'Doe'. The new value for the phone column is '555-555-1234'.

Deleting Data

The DELETE statement is used to remove rows from a table. The basic syntax of the DELETE statement is as follows:

```
DELETE FROM table_name
WHERE condition;
```

In this syntax, table_name is the name of the table from which you want to delete the data.

The WHERE clause specifies which rows you want to delete. If you omit the WHERE clause, all rows in the table will be deleted.

Let's take a look at an example:

```sql
DELETE FROM employees
WHERE last_name = 'Doe';
```

In this example, we are deleting all rows from the employees table where the last_name column is 'Doe'.

It is important to be cautious when deleting data from a table because once it is deleted, it cannot be recovered. You can use transactions to ensure that the changes are committed only if all the steps are completed successfully.

Inserting, updating, and deleting data are essential operations for managing a database. The INSERT statement is used to insert new rows into a table, the UPDATE statement is used to modify existing rows, and the DELETE statement is used to remove rows from a table. These operations are performed using SQL statements, and can be executed using various tools or programming languages. It is important to be cautious when performing these operations to avoid unintended consequences, and to use transactions to ensure data integrity.

Best practices for inserting, updating, and deleting data

To ensure that data is inserted, updated, and deleted correctly and efficiently, it is important to follow best practices. Here are some tips:

Use parameterized queries: Parameterized queries allow you to pass values to a SQL statement as parameters, rather than concatenating values directly into the query string. This can help prevent SQL injection attacks and improve performance.

Use transactions: Transactions allow you to group a series of database operations into a single unit of work. This can help ensure data consistency and integrity, and can also help improve performance by reducing the number of round-trips to the database.

Use indexes: Indexes can help improve query performance by allowing the database to quickly locate the rows that match a given criteria. However, be careful not to over-index, as too many indexes can actually slow down performance.

Normalize your data: Normalizing your data can help improve data integrity and reduce data duplication. This can make it easier to insert, update, and delete data, as well as perform queries.

Use triggers sparingly: Triggers are special types of stored procedures that are automatically executed when certain events occur, such as when a row is inserted, updated, or deleted.

While triggers can be useful in certain situations, they can also be complex and difficult to maintain, so use them sparingly.

Inserting, updating, and deleting data are essential operations for managing a database. By following best practices such as using parameterized queries, transactions, indexes, normalized data, and triggers sparingly, you can ensure that these operations are performed correctly and efficiently. It is also important to test your queries thoroughly to ensure that they work as expected and to be cautious when performing these operations to avoid unintended consequences.

Tools for inserting, updating, and deleting data

There are many tools available for inserting, updating, and deleting data in SQL Server. Here are some of the most commonly used tools:

SQL Server Management Studio (SSMS): SSMS is a graphical user interface (GUI) tool that allows you to interact with SQL Server. You can use SSMS to create and modify tables, insert, update, and delete data, and perform many other database management tasks.

SQLCMD: SQLCMD is a command-line tool that allows you to execute SQL statements and scripts from the command prompt. You can use SQLCMD to automate tasks, such as inserting data from a text file, or to execute scripts that perform multiple operations.

Visual Studio: If you are developing applications that use SQL Server, you can use Visual Studio to create data connections, insert, update, and delete data, and perform many other database-related tasks. Visual Studio also provides tools for designing and developing SQL Server databases.

PowerShell: PowerShell is a command-line shell and scripting language that is used to automate administrative tasks in Windows. You can use PowerShell to automate tasks, such as inserting, updating, and deleting data, by executing SQL statements or scripts.

SQL Server provides many tools for inserting, updating, and deleting data, including graphical user interfaces, command-line tools, and programming tools. Depending on your needs and preferences, you can choose the tool that best suits your requirements. When using these tools, be sure to follow best practices and test your queries thoroughly to ensure that they work as expected.

Error handling for inserting, updating, and deleting data

When performing operations that insert, update, or delete data, it is important to handle errors appropriately. Here are some best practices for error handling:

Use try-catch blocks: In SQL Server, you can use try-catch blocks to handle errors that occur during database operations. A try-catch block allows you to catch errors and take appropriate action, such as rolling back a transaction or displaying an error message.

Check for errors after each operation: When performing a series of database operations, it is important to check for errors after each operation. This allows you to catch errors early and take appropriate action.

Log errors: Logging errors can help you identify and diagnose problems with your database operations. You can log errors to the Windows Event Log, to a file, or to a database table.

Use error codes: Error codes can help you identify the type of error that occurred and take appropriate action. SQL Server provides a list of error codes and descriptions that you can use to identify errors.

Use transactions: Transactions can help ensure data consistency and integrity, and can also help with error handling. By using transactions, you can roll back a series of operations if an error occurs, rather than committing partial changes to the database.

Error handling is an important aspect of inserting, updating, and deleting data in SQL Server. By using try-catch blocks, checking for errors after each operation, logging errors, using error codes, and using transactions, you can ensure that errors are handled appropriately and that your database operations are performed correctly and efficiently.

Performance considerations for inserting, updating, and deleting data

When inserting, updating, or deleting large amounts of data in SQL Server, performance can be a concern. Here are some best practices for improving performance:

Use batching: If you need to insert, update, or delete a large number of records, you can improve performance by using batching. Instead of performing the operation on all records at once, you can break the operation into smaller batches and execute them separately.

Use stored procedures: Stored procedures can improve performance by reducing network traffic and reducing the amount of time required to parse and optimize queries. By using stored procedures, you can also take advantage of parameterized queries and caching.

Use indexes: Indexes can improve performance by allowing SQL Server to locate and retrieve data more quickly. By creating indexes on columns that are frequently used in WHERE clauses, you can improve query performance.

Use constraints: Constraints can improve performance by ensuring data integrity and reducing the amount of time required to check data consistency. By using constraints, you can also improve query performance by allowing SQL Server to use more efficient execution plans.

Use bulk operations: If you need to insert, update, or delete a large number of records, you can improve performance by using bulk operations. SQL Server provides several bulk operations, including BULK INSERT, BCP, and OPENROWSET.

When inserting, updating, or deleting large amounts of data in SQL Server, performance can be a concern. By using batching, stored procedures, indexes, constraints, and bulk operations, you can improve performance and ensure that your database operations are performed efficiently. Additionally, it is important to monitor performance and make adjustments as necessary to optimize performance.

Conclusion

Inserting, updating, and deleting data are essential operations in SQL Server. Understanding how to perform these operations correctly and efficiently is crucial for developers who work with databases. By following the best practices outlined in this chapter, you can ensure that your database operations are performed correctly and efficiently.

When inserting data, it is important to use explicit column lists, parameterized queries, and transactions to ensure data integrity and prevent SQL injection attacks. When updating data, it is important to use the WHERE clause to specify which records to update, and to be aware of the potential for race conditions. When deleting data, it is important to use the WHERE clause to specify which records to delete, and to be aware of the potential for cascading deletes.

Error handling and performance considerations are also important aspects of inserting, updating, and deleting data in SQL Server. By using try-catch blocks, checking for errors after each operation, logging errors, using error codes, and using transactions, you can ensure that errors are handled appropriately. By using batching, stored procedures, indexes, constraints, and bulk operations, you can improve performance and ensure that your database operations are performed efficiently.

In summary, inserting, updating, and deleting data in SQL Server requires careful consideration of data integrity, security, error handling, and performance. By following the best practices outlined in this chapter, you can ensure that your database operations are performed correctly and efficiently, and that your data is safe and secure.

Chapter 2.0 - Selecting and Filtering Data

Chapter 2.1 - Using SELECT statements to retrieve data from a database

SQL Server is a powerful relational database management system that allows developers to store, manage, and retrieve data efficiently. One of the most important tasks that developers perform with SQL Server is retrieving data from databases. In this chapter, we will discuss how to use SELECT statements to retrieve data from a SQL Server database.

The SELECT Statement

The SELECT statement is the primary tool that developers use to retrieve data from a SQL Server database. The basic syntax of a SELECT statement is:

```
SELECT column1, column2, ...
FROM table_name;
```

In this syntax, the SELECT keyword is followed by a comma-separated list of columns that you want to retrieve from the specified table. The FROM keyword is used to specify the table from which you want to retrieve data.

For example, the following SELECT statement retrieves all columns from a customers table:

```
SELECT *
FROM customers;
```

In this example, the * symbol is used as a shorthand for all columns in the customers table. This query will retrieve all data from the customers table.

Retrieving Specific Columns

Often, developers only need to retrieve specific columns from a table, rather than all columns. In these cases, you can specify the column names in the SELECT statement, separated by commas.

For example, the following SELECT statement retrieves only the first_name and last_name columns from a customers table:

```
SELECT first_name, last_name
FROM customers;
```

In this example, the SELECT statement specifies two columns: first_name and last_name. The query will retrieve only these two columns from the customers table.

Filtering Data with WHERE Clause

The WHERE clause is used to filter data based on specific conditions. The basic syntax for the WHERE clause is:

```
SELECT column1, column2, ...
FROM table_name
WHERE condition;
```

In this syntax, the WHERE keyword is followed by a condition that specifies the filtering criteria. Only the rows that meet the specified condition will be retrieved.

For example, the following SELECT statement retrieves all columns from a customers table where the city is 'New York':

```
SELECT *
FROM customers
WHERE city = 'New York';
```

In this example, the WHERE clause specifies the condition that the city column must be equal to 'New York'. The query will retrieve all columns from the customers table where the city is 'New York'.

Retrieving Distinct Rows

Sometimes, a table may contain duplicate rows, which can make data analysis more challenging. To retrieve only distinct rows from a table, you can use the DISTINCT keyword in the SELECT statement.

For example, the following SELECT statement retrieves all distinct values of the state column from a customers table:

```
SELECT DISTINCT state
FROM customers;
```

In this example, the SELECT statement specifies the DISTINCT keyword before the state column. The query will retrieve only distinct values of the state column from the customers table.

Sorting Data with ORDER BY Clause

The ORDER BY clause is used to sort the retrieved data based on one or more columns. The basic syntax for the ORDER BY clause is:

```
SELECT column1, column2, ...
FROM table_name
ORDER BY column1 [ASC|DESC], column2 [ASC|DESC], ...;
```

In this syntax, the ORDER BY keyword is followed by one or more columns that you want to sort by. You can specify the sorting order for each column as ASC (ascending) or DESC (descending).

For example, the following SELECT statement retrieves all columns from a customers table, sorted by last_name in ascending order:

```
SELECT *
FROM customers
ORDER BY last_name ASC;
```

In this example, the ORDER BY clause specifies the last_name column and the ASC keyword, which means that the data will be sorted in ascending order by the last_name column.

Limiting Rows with LIMIT Clause

Sometimes, you may want to retrieve only a certain number of rows from a table. In these cases, you can use the LIMIT clause in the SELECT statement.

The basic syntax for the LIMIT clause is:

```
SELECT column1, column2, ...
FROM table_name
LIMIT number_of_rows;
```

In this syntax, the LIMIT keyword is followed by the number of rows that you want to retrieve.

For example, the following SELECT statement retrieves the first 10 rows from a customers table:

```
SELECT *
FROM customers
LIMIT 10;
```

In this example, the LIMIT clause specifies that only the first 10 rows of the customers table should be retrieved.

Combining SELECT, WHERE, ORDER BY, and LIMIT Clauses

In many cases, you will need to combine the SELECT, WHERE, ORDER BY, and LIMIT clauses to retrieve data from a database. Here's an example of a SELECT statement that uses all four clauses:

```
SELECT first_name, last_name, email
FROM customers
WHERE city = 'New York'
ORDER BY last_name ASC
LIMIT 10;
```

In this example, the SELECT statement retrieves only the first_name, last_name, and email columns from the customers table, where the city is 'New York'. The data is sorted by last_name in ascending order, and only the first 10 rows are retrieved.

Conclusion

In this chapter, we have discussed how to use SELECT statements to retrieve data from a SQL Server database. We have covered the basic syntax of the SELECT statement, retrieving specific columns, filtering data with the WHERE clause, retrieving distinct rows, sorting data with the ORDER BY clause, limiting rows with the LIMIT clause, and combining these clauses in a single SELECT statement. Understanding how to use these clauses effectively is essential for any developer working with SQL Server.

Chapter 2.2 - Filtering and Sorting Data using WHERE and ORDER BY Clauses

SQL Server provides several powerful tools for filtering and sorting data in a database. Two of the most commonly used tools are the WHERE and ORDER BY clauses. These clauses allow you to retrieve only the data that you need, and to sort that data in a way that makes sense for your application. In this chapter, we will explore how to use the WHERE and ORDER BY clauses to filter and sort data in SQL Server.

Filtering Data using the WHERE Clause

The WHERE clause is used to filter data based on a specified condition. This clause is used in conjunction with the SELECT statement to retrieve only the data that meets the specified condition. The basic syntax of the WHERE clause is:

```
SELECT column1, column2, ...
FROM table_name
WHERE condition;
```

In this syntax, "column1, column2, ..." are the names of the columns that you want to retrieve data from. "table_name" is the name of the table that contains the data. And "condition" is the condition that the data must meet in order to be retrieved. The condition can be any valid SQL expression, and can include operators such as "=", "<", ">", and "LIKE".

Let's take a look at some examples of using the WHERE clause to filter data:

Example 1: Retrieving all customers from a customers table whose last name is "Smith".

```
SELECT *
FROM customers
WHERE last_name = 'Smith';
```

In this example, we are retrieving all columns from the customers table where the last_name column equals "Smith". This query will return all customers whose last name is "Smith".

Example 2: Retrieving all orders from an orders table where the order date is between '2020-01-01' and '2020-12-31'.

```
SELECT *
FROM orders
WHERE order_date BETWEEN '2020-01-01' AND '2020-12-31';
```

In this example, we are retrieving all columns from the orders table where the order_date column is between '2020-01-01' and '2020-12-31'. This query will return all orders that were placed in the year 2020.

Example 3: Retrieving all products from a products table whose name contains the word "shirt".

```
SELECT *
FROM products
WHERE name LIKE '%shirt%';
```

In this example, we are retrieving all columns from the products table where the name column contains the word "shirt". The "%" symbol is used as a wildcard character to match any number of characters before or after the word "shirt". This query will return all products whose name contains the word "shirt", such as "T-shirt" and "Dress shirt".

Sorting Data using the ORDER BY Clause

The ORDER BY clause is used to sort data based on one or more columns in a table. This clause is used in conjunction with the SELECT statement to retrieve data that is sorted in a specific order. The basic syntax of the ORDER BY clause is:

```
SELECT column1, column2, ...
FROM table_name
ORDER BY column1 [ASC|DESC], column2 [ASC|DESC], ...;
```

In this syntax, "column1, column2, ..." are the names of the columns that you want to retrieve data from. "table_name" is the name of the table that contains the data. The ORDER BY clause specifies the columns that the data should be sorted by, and whether the sorting should be done in ascending (ASC) or descending (DESC) order. You can specify multiple columns to sort by, and each column can be sorted in a different order.

Let's take a look at some examples of using the ORDER BY clause to sort data:

Example 1: Retrieving all customers from a customers table, sorted by last name in ascending order.

```
SELECT *
FROM customers
ORDER BY last_name ASC;
```

In this example, we are retrieving all columns from the customers table, and sorting the data by the last_name column in ascending order. This query will return all customers in alphabetical order by their last name.

Example 2: Retrieving all products from a products table, sorted by price in descending order.

```
SELECT *
FROM products
ORDER BY price DESC;
```

In this example, we are retrieving all columns from the products table, and sorting the data by the price column in descending order. This query will return all products in descending order by their price, with the most expensive products appearing first.

Example 3: Retrieving all orders from an orders table, sorted by customer ID in ascending order and then by order date in descending order.

```
SELECT *
FROM orders
ORDER BY customer_id ASC, order_date DESC;
```

In this example, we are retrieving all columns from the orders table, and sorting the data first by the customer_id column in ascending order, and then by the order_date column in descending order. This query will return all orders sorted by customer ID, and then by order date within each customer.

Combining the WHERE and ORDER BY Clauses

You can use the WHERE and ORDER BY clauses together to filter and sort data based on specific conditions. The basic syntax for combining these clauses is:

```
SELECT column1, column2, ...
FROM table_name
WHERE condition
ORDER BY column1 [ASC|DESC], column2 [ASC|DESC], ...;
```

In this syntax, the WHERE clause is used to filter data based on a specific condition, and the ORDER BY clause is used to sort the filtered data based on one or more columns.

Let's take a look at an example of combining the WHERE and ORDER BY clauses:

Example: Retrieving all orders from an orders table where the order date is between '2020-01-01' and '2020-12-31', sorted by order date in descending order.

```
SELECT *
```

```
FROM orders
WHERE order_date BETWEEN '2020-01-01' AND '2020-12-31'
ORDER BY order_date DESC;
```

In this example, we are retrieving all columns from the orders table where the order_date column is between '2020-01-01' and '2020-12-31', and sorting the filtered data by the order_date column in descending order. This query will return all orders placed in the year 2020, sorted by order date with the most recent orders appearing first.

Conclusion

Filtering and sorting data are two essential tasks in SQL Server, and the WHERE and ORDER BY clauses are two powerful tools that can be used to accomplish these tasks. By using the WHERE clause, you can retrieve only the data that you need based on specific conditions. And by using the ORDER BY clause, you can sort the retrieved data in a way that makes sense for your application. By combining these clauses, you can filter and sort data based on specific conditions, allowing you to retrieve the data that you need quickly and efficiently.

Chapter 2.3 - Joining tables and working with multiple tables

As a software developer working with SQL Server, you will often need to retrieve data from multiple tables. To do this, you will need to join the tables together in your SQL statements. In this chapter, we will cover the basics of table joins and provide examples of how to use them in your queries.

What is a table join?

A table join is a SQL operation that combines two or more tables into a single table. The resulting table contains all of the columns from the original tables, as well as any additional columns that you specify in your SQL statement.

Table joins are necessary when you need to retrieve data that is spread across multiple tables. For example, if you have a customers table and an orders table, you might need to join the two tables together to retrieve all of the orders for a specific customer.

There are several types of table joins, including inner joins, outer joins, and cross joins. In this chapter, we will focus on inner joins and left outer joins, as these are the most commonly used joins in SQL Server.

Inner joins

An inner join returns only the rows that have matching values in both tables. In other words, if a row exists in one table but not in the other, it will not be included in the result set.

The basic syntax for an inner join is as follows:

```
SELECT column1, column2, ...
FROM table1
INNER JOIN table2 ON table1.column = table2.column;
```

In this syntax, the INNER JOIN keyword specifies that we want to perform an inner join, and the ON keyword specifies the condition that we want to use to join the tables.

Here is an example of an inner join that joins a customers table with an orders table:

```sql
SELECT customers.first_name, customers.last_name, orders.order_date
FROM customers
INNER JOIN orders ON customers.customer_id = orders.customer_id;
```

In this example, we are retrieving the first name and last name of each customer, as well as the order date for each order. The two tables are joined on the customer_id column, which is a common column between the two tables.

Left Outer Joins

A left outer join returns all of the rows from the left table and any matching rows from the right table. If there are no matching rows in the right table, the result set will contain NULL values for the right table columns.

The basic syntax for a left outer join is as follows:

```sql
SELECT column1, column2, ...
FROM table1
LEFT OUTER JOIN table2 ON table1.column = table2.column;
```

In this syntax, the LEFT OUTER JOIN keyword specifies that we want to perform a left outer join.

Here is an example of a left outer join that joins a customers table with an orders table:

```sql
SELECT customers.first_name, customers.last_name, orders.order_date
FROM customers
LEFT OUTER JOIN orders ON customers.customer_id = orders.customer_id;
```

In this example, we are retrieving the first name and last name of each customer, as well as the order date for each order. The left outer join ensures that all of the customers are included in the result set, even if they have not placed any orders.

Combining joins with other clauses

You can combine table joins with other SQL clauses, such as WHERE and ORDER BY, to further refine your queries.

For example, here is a query that combines a left outer join with a WHERE clause to retrieve all customers who have not placed any orders:

```sql
SELECT customers.first_name, customers.last_name
FROM customers
LEFT OUTER JOIN orders ON customers.customer_id = orders.customer_id
WHERE orders.order_id IS NULL;
```

In this example, we are using a WHERE clause to filter the result set to only include customers who have not placed any orders. The left outer join ensures that all of the customers are included in the result set, even if they have not placed any orders.

You can also use table aliases to make your SQL statements more readable. An alias is a short name that you can give to a table or column, which you can then use in place of the full table or column name.

Here is an example of a query that uses table aliases:

```sql
SELECT c.first_name, c.last_name, o.order_date
FROM customers c
LEFT OUTER JOIN orders o ON c.customer_id = o.customer_id;
```

In this example, we have given the customers table an alias of c, and the orders table an alias of o. We can then use these aliases in place of the full table names throughout the query.

Conclusion

Table joins are an essential part of working with multiple tables in SQL Server. By using inner joins and left outer joins, you can retrieve data that is spread across multiple tables and combine it into a single result set.

When using table joins, it is important to remember to specify the condition that you want to use to join the tables, and to use table aliases to make your SQL statements more readable.

In the next chapter, we will cover subqueries and how you can use them to further refine your SQL queries.

Chapter 2.4 - Understanding APPLY Statements in SQL Server

SQL Server's APPLY operator is a powerful tool that allows you to perform complex operations on data within a query. With APPLY, you can join a table to a table-valued function, allowing you to perform calculations or transformations on the data. In this chapter, we will explore how to use APPLY statements in SQL Server to simplify complex queries and improve performance.

What is an APPLY Statement?

An APPLY statement is a type of join that allows you to join a table to a table-valued function. There are two types of APPLY statements in SQL Server: CROSS APPLY and OUTER APPLY.

CROSS APPLY returns only the rows from the table-valued function that match the rows in the table being joined. OUTER APPLY, on the other hand, returns all the rows from the table being joined, along with any matching rows from the table-valued function. If there are no matching rows in the table-valued function, OUTER APPLY returns NULL values.

Using CROSS APPLY Statements

Let's start with a simple example of using CROSS APPLY statements in SQL Server. Suppose we have two tables: Orders and OrderDetails. The Orders table contains information about orders, such as the order date and customer ID, while the OrderDetails table contains information about the items ordered, such as the item name and price.

To get a list of all orders along with their associated items, we can use a CROSS APPLY statement to join the Orders table to a table-valued function that returns the items associated with each order. Here's what the query might look like:

```sql
SELECT o.OrderID, o.OrderDate, od.ItemName, od.ItemPrice
FROM Orders o
CROSS APPLY (
    SELECT ItemName, ItemPrice
    FROM OrderDetails
    WHERE OrderID = o.OrderID
) od
```

In this example, the table-valued function is a subquery that returns the items associated with each order. The APPLY operator joins the Orders table to the subquery, allowing us to get a list of all orders along with their associated items.

Note that we are using the OrderID column from the Orders table to filter the results of the subquery. This ensures that we only get the items associated with each order, rather than all the items in the OrderDetails table.

Using OUTER APPLY Statements

Next, let's look at an example of using OUTER APPLY statements in SQL Server. Suppose we have a table of employees, along with a table of employee phone numbers. We want to get a list of all employees, along with their phone numbers, even if they don't have a phone number listed in the phone number table.

To accomplish this, we can use an OUTER APPLY statement to join the employees table to the phone number table. Here's what the query might look like:

```sql
SELECT e.EmployeeID, e.FirstName, e.LastName, p.PhoneNumber
FROM Employees e
OUTER APPLY (
    SELECT TOP 1 PhoneNumber
    FROM EmployeePhoneNumbers
    WHERE EmployeeID = e.EmployeeID
    ORDER BY PhoneNumberID ASC
) p
```

In this example, the table-valued function is a subquery that returns the first phone number associated with each employee. Since we are using OUTER APPLY, we will get all the rows from the Employees table, along with any matching rows from the subquery. If an employee does not have a phone number listed in the phone number table, the PhoneNumber column will contain a NULL value.

Note that we are using the EmployeeID column from the Employees table to filter the results of the subquery. This ensures that we only get the phone number associated with each employee, rather than all the phone numbers in the EmployeePhoneNumbers table.

Using APPLY Statements with User-Defined Functions

So far, we have been using subqueries as the table-valued functions in our APPLY statements. However, we can also use user-defined functions (UDFs) as the table-valued functions in our APPLY statements. This allows us to perform more complex calculations or transformations on the data.

Let's look at an example of using a UDF in an APPLY statement in SQL Server. Suppose we have a table of products, along with a table of orders. We want to get a list of all products, along with the total number of orders and the total revenue generated by each product.

To accomplish this, we can create a UDF that takes a product ID as a parameter and returns the total number of orders and the total revenue generated by that product. Here's what the UDF might look like:

```sql
CREATE FUNCTION dbo.GetProductStats (@ProductID INT)
RETURNS TABLE
AS
RETURN (
    SELECT COUNT(*) AS NumOrders, SUM(OrderAmount) AS TotalRevenue
    FROM Orders
    WHERE ProductID = @ProductID
)
```

In this example, the UDF takes a product ID as a parameter and returns a table with two columns: NumOrders and TotalRevenue. The subquery in the UDF calculates the total number of orders and the total revenue generated by the product with the specified ID.

Now, we can use the UDF in an OUTER APPLY statement to get the product statistics for each product. Here's what the query might look like:

```sql
SELECT p.ProductID, p.ProductName, s.NumOrders, s.TotalRevenue
FROM Products p
OUTER APPLY dbo.GetProductStats(p.ProductID) s
```

In this example, we are using OUTER APPLY to join the Products table to the GetProductStats UDF. The UDF returns the product statistics for each product, which are then joined to the Products table using OUTER APPLY.

Note that we are passing the ProductID column from the Products table as a parameter to the GetProductStats UDF. This ensures that we get the product statistics for each product, rather than all the product statistics in the Orders table.

Conclusion

In this chapter, we have explored how to use APPLY statements in SQL Server to join tables to table-valued functions or user-defined functions. APPLY statements are a powerful tool that can simplify complex queries and improve performance. By using APPLY statements, you can perform calculations or transformations on the data within a query, making it easier to analyze and understand. Whether you are a beginner or an experienced SQL developer, APPLY statements are an essential skill to have in your toolbox.

In addition, APPLY statements can also be used in more advanced scenarios, such as recursive queries. Recursive queries involve querying a table that has a relationship with itself, such as a hierarchy or a network. APPLY statements can help simplify these queries and make them more efficient.

Let's look at an example of using an APPLY statement in a recursive query. Suppose we have a table of employees, along with their managers. We want to create a hierarchical structure that shows each employee and their direct and indirect managers.

To accomplish this, we can use a recursive CTE (common table expression) and an OUTER APPLY statement. Here's what the query might look like:

```sql
WITH EmployeeHierarchy (EmployeeID, ManagerID, EmployeeName,
ManagerName, Level)
AS
(
    SELECT e.EmployeeID, e.ManagerID, e.EmployeeName, m.EmployeeName AS
ManagerName, 0 AS Level
    FROM Employees e
    LEFT JOIN Employees m ON e.ManagerID = m.EmployeeID


    UNION ALL


    SELECT e.EmployeeID, e.ManagerID, e.EmployeeName, m.ManagerName,
eh.Level + 1
    FROM Employees e
    INNER JOIN EmployeeHierarchy eh ON e.ManagerID = eh.EmployeeID
    LEFT JOIN Employees m ON e.ManagerID = m.EmployeeID
)
SELECT EmployeeID, EmployeeName, ManagerName, Level
FROM EmployeeHierarchy
OUTER APPLY
(
    SELECT TOP 1 ManagerName
    FROM EmployeeHierarchy eh2
    WHERE eh2.EmployeeID = EmployeeHierarchy.ManagerID
    ORDER BY Level DESC
) Manager
```

In this example, we are using a recursive CTE to create a hierarchical structure of employees and managers. The CTE starts with the base case of each employee and their immediate manager, and then recursively joins to the EmployeeHierarchy CTE to include each employee's indirect managers.

We are also using OUTER APPLY to get the name of each employee's top-level manager. The subquery in the OUTER APPLY statement uses the EmployeeHierarchy CTE to find the top-level manager for each employee, based on the maximum level in the hierarchy.

Note that this query can also be written using a LEFT JOIN instead of an OUTER APPLY. However, using OUTER APPLY can sometimes be more efficient, especially when dealing with large datasets.

Conclusion

In this chapter, we have explored how to use APPLY statements in more advanced scenarios, such as recursive queries. By using APPLY statements, you can simplify complex queries and make them more efficient. Whether you are a beginner or an experienced SQL developer, APPLY statements are an essential skill to have in your toolbox.

In conclusion, APPLY statements are a powerful tool in SQL Server that can help simplify complex queries and improve performance. By using APPLY statements, you can join tables to table-valued functions or user-defined functions, perform calculations or transformations on the data, and even handle more advanced scenarios such as recursive queries. Whether you are a beginner or an experienced SQL developer, APPLY statements are an essential skill to have in your toolbox.

Chapter 3 - Advanced SQL Server Techniques

Chapter 3.1 - Grouping and Aggregating Data Using GROUP BY and HAVING Clauses

In SQL Server, you can use the GROUP BY and HAVING clauses to group and aggregate data in a query. Grouping and aggregating data allows you to summarize large amounts of data and extract meaningful information from it.

In this chapter, we will cover how to use the GROUP BY and HAVING clauses in SQL Server, and provide examples of how you can use them to group and aggregate data.

GROUP BY Clause

The GROUP BY clause is used to group the results of a query by one or more columns. When you group data using the GROUP BY clause, the data is divided into subsets based on the values in the specified columns.

Here is an example of a query that uses the GROUP BY clause:

```
SELECT country, COUNT(*) as total_customers
FROM customers
GROUP BY country;
```

In this example, we are grouping the results by the country column in the customers table. We are also using the COUNT(*) function to count the number of customers in each country. The result of this query would be a list of countries and the total number of customers in each country.

You can also group data by multiple columns by including them in the GROUP BY clause:

```
SELECT country, city, COUNT(*) as total_customers
FROM customers
GROUP BY country, city;
```

In this example, we are grouping the results by both the country and city columns in the customers table. The result of this query would be a list of countries and cities, and the total number of customers in each city within each country.

Aggregating Data with Functions

When you use the GROUP BY clause, you typically also use aggregation functions to calculate values for each group. Aggregation functions take a set of values as input and return a single value as output.

Here are some of the most commonly used aggregation functions in SQL Server:

COUNT(): returns the number of rows in a group.
SUM(): returns the sum of a numeric column in a group.
AVG(): returns the average of a numeric column in a group.
MIN(): returns the minimum value of a column in a group.
MAX(): returns the maximum value of a column in a group.
Here is an example of a query that uses the SUM() function to calculate the total revenue for each customer:

```
SELECT customer_id, SUM(total_price) as total_revenue
FROM orders
GROUP BY customer_id;
```

In this example, we are grouping the results by the customer_id column in the orders table. We are also using the SUM() function to calculate the total revenue for each customer. The result of this query would be a list of customer IDs and their total revenue.

HAVING Clause

The HAVING clause is used to filter groups based on a specified condition. The HAVING clause is similar to the WHERE clause, but is used to filter groups instead of individual rows.

Here is an example of a query that uses the HAVING clause:

```
SELECT country, AVG(total_price) as avg_order_price
FROM orders
JOIN customers ON orders.customer_id = customers.customer_id
GROUP BY country
HAVING AVG(total_price) > 1000;
```

In this example, we are using the JOIN clause to join the orders and customers tables. We are grouping the results by country, and using the AVG() function to calculate the average order price for each country. We are then using the HAVING clause to filter the results to only show countries where the average order price is greater than 1000.

Conclusion

In this chapter, we have covered how to use the GROUP BY and HAVING clauses in SQL Server to group and aggregate data in a query. We have also provided examples of how to use aggregation functions to calculate values for each group, and how to use the HAVING clause to filter groups based on a specified condition.

Grouping and aggregating data is an essential skill for any SQL developer. By using the GROUP BY and HAVING clauses, you can extract meaningful information from large amounts of data, and gain insights that can help inform business decisions.

As with any SQL query, it is important to test your queries and make sure they return the expected results. It is also important to understand the performance implications of grouping and aggregating large amounts of data, and to optimize your queries accordingly.

By mastering the GROUP BY and HAVING clauses, you can take your SQL skills to the next level and become a more effective and efficient SQL developer.

Chapter - 3.2 - Creating and using subqueries

As a software developer, you understand that data is at the heart of every application. Whether it's retrieving, updating, or manipulating data, SQL Server provides powerful tools to help you manage your data efficiently. One such tool is subqueries, which are a fundamental concept in SQL Server that allows you to nest queries within other queries. In this chapter, we will explore how to create and use subqueries to harness the full power of SQL Server.

Understanding Subqueries

A subquery is a query that is embedded within another query, typically enclosed in parentheses and used within the larger query's main body. The result of a subquery is used as an input to the outer query, allowing you to perform complex operations and retrieve data in a more refined and precise manner. Subqueries can be used in various parts of a SQL statement, such as the SELECT, FROM, WHERE, and HAVING clauses, and can even be used in conjunction with other subqueries to create intricate queries.

One of the key benefits of using subqueries is that they allow you to break down complex problems into smaller, more manageable parts. Instead of writing a single monolithic query that tries to accomplish everything at once, you can break it down into smaller, more focused subqueries that are easier to understand, test, and optimize. Subqueries also provide a way to retrieve data from one table based on the values of another table, allowing you to perform operations such as filtering, joining, and aggregation in a more dynamic and flexible manner.

Creating Subqueries

To create a subquery in SQL Server, you simply need to include a complete SELECT statement within another query. The syntax for a subquery is as follows:

```
SELECT column1, column2, ...
FROM table1
WHERE column1 = (SELECT column1 FROM table2 WHERE condition);
```

In this example, the subquery is enclosed in parentheses and is used as an input to the WHERE clause of the outer query. The result of the subquery is compared to the value of column1 in table1 to determine if the row should be included in the final result set. Note that a subquery must always return a single value, such as a scalar value or a single-row result set, to be used in this manner.

You can also use subqueries to retrieve multiple rows as a result set, and use them in other parts of your query, such as the SELECT and FROM clauses. For example, you can use a subquery in the SELECT clause to perform calculations or retrieve additional information based on the values of the main query. Here's an example:

```sql
SELECT column1, column2, (SELECT MAX(column3) FROM table2 WHERE column1
= table1.column1) AS max_value
FROM table1;
```

In this example, the subquery retrieves the maximum value of column3 from table2 for each row in table1 that matches the condition column1 = table1.column1. The result of the subquery is then included as a calculated column named max_value in the final result set.

Using Subqueries in WHERE Clauses

One of the most common use cases for subqueries is to use them in the WHERE clause to filter data based on the results of another query. This allows you to perform complex filtering operations that are not possible with simple comparisons or logical operators. Here's an example:

```sql
SELECT column1, column2
FROM table1
WHERE column1 IN (SELECT column1 FROM table2 WHERE condition);
```

In this example, the subquery retrieves a list of values for column1 from table2 based on a condition, and the outer query retrieves rows from table1 where column1 matches any of the values retrieved by the subquery. This is equivalent to saying "retrieve all rows from table1 where column1 is present in the list of values retrieved by the subquery".

You can also use other comparison operators such as <, >, <=, >=, <>, and LIKE in combination with subqueries to perform more complex filtering. For example:

```sql
SELECT column1, column2
FROM table1
WHERE column1 > (SELECT AVG(column1) FROM table2);
```

In this example, the subquery calculates the average value of column1 from table2, and the outer query retrieves rows from table1 where the value of column1 is greater than the calculated average.

It's important to note that subqueries can have an impact on performance, especially when dealing with large tables or complex queries. Subqueries are executed sequentially, meaning that the outer query is dependent on the results of the subquery, and the subquery may need to be executed multiple times for each row in the outer query. Therefore, it's crucial to optimize your subqueries and use them judiciously to avoid performance issues.

Using Subqueries in the FROM Clause

In addition to using subqueries in the WHERE clause, you can also use them in the FROM clause to treat the result of a subquery as a virtual table that can be used as a data source in the outer query. This allows you to join, filter, and aggregate data from multiple tables in a single query. Here's an example:

```
SELECT column1, SUM(column2)
FROM (SELECT column1, column2 FROM table1 WHERE condition) AS subquery
GROUP BY column1;
```

In this example, the subquery retrieves a subset of columns from table1 based on a condition, and the outer query treats the result of the subquery as a virtual table named subquery that can be used in the GROUP BY clause to perform aggregation.

You can also use subqueries in the FROM clause to perform complex joins and filtering operations. For example:

```
SELECT column1, column2
FROM table1
JOIN (SELECT column1 FROM table2 WHERE condition) AS subquery ON
table1.column1 = subquery.column1;
```

In this example, the subquery retrieves a list of values for column1 from table2 based on a condition, and the outer query performs a join with table1 based on the matching values of column1.

Using Subqueries in the SELECT Clause

Another powerful use of subqueries is to include them in the SELECT clause to perform calculations or retrieve additional information based on the values of the main query. This allows you to dynamically calculate values or retrieve related data without having to join multiple tables or perform complex calculations in the main query. Here's an example:

```
SELECT column1, column2, (SELECT COUNT(*) FROM table2 WHERE column1 =
table1.column1) AS count
FROM table1;
```

In this example, the subquery calculates the count of rows in table2 that match the condition column1 = table1.column1 for each row in table1, and the result of the subquery is included as a calculated column named count in the final result set.

You can also use subqueries in the SELECT clause to perform other calculations such as arithmetic operations, string concatenation, and date manipulations. For example:

```sql
SELECT column1, column2, column3 * (SELECT AVG(column3) FROM table2) AS calculated_value
FROM table1;
```

In this example, the subquery calculates the average value of column3 from table2, and the outer query multiplies the value of column3 in each row of table1 with the calculated average, resulting in a calculated column named calculated_value in the final result set.

Advanced Subquery Techniques

Subqueries can also be combined with other SQL features to perform advanced operations and achieve more complex functionality. Here are some additional techniques you can use with subqueries:

Subqueries with EXISTS and NOT EXISTS:

You can use subqueries in combination with the EXISTS and NOT EXISTS operators to check for the existence or non-existence of rows in a subquery. For example:

```sql
SELECT column1, column2
FROM table1
WHERE EXISTS (SELECT * FROM table2 WHERE column1 = table1.column1);
```

In this example, the subquery checks if there are any rows in table2 that match the condition column1 = table1.column1, and the outer query retrieves rows from table1 where the subquery returns true.

Subqueries with IN and NOT IN:

You can use subqueries in combination with the IN and NOT IN operators to check if a value exists or does not exist in a list of values retrieved by a subquery. For example:

```sql
SELECT column1, column2
FROM table1
WHERE column1 NOT IN (SELECT column1 FROM table2);
```

In this example, the subquery retrieves a list of values for column1 from table2, and the outer query retrieves rows from table1 where the value of column1 is not present in the list retrieved by the subquery.

Correlated Subqueries:

Correlated subqueries are subqueries that refer to columns from the outer query, allowing you to perform operations that depend on values from the outer query. For example:

```
SELECT column1, column2
FROM table1
WHERE column2 > (SELECT AVG(column2) FROM table1 WHERE column1 =
table1.column1);
```

In this example, the subquery calculates the average value of column2 for each unique value of column1 in table1, and the outer query retrieves rows from table1 where the value of column2 is greater than the calculated average for the corresponding column1 value.

Subqueries in INSERT, UPDATE, and DELETE Statements:

Subqueries can also be used in INSERT, UPDATE, and DELETE statements to perform operations based on the result of a subquery. For example:

```
INSERT INTO table1 (column1, column2)
SELECT column1, column2
FROM table2
WHERE condition;
```

In this example, the subquery retrieves values for column1 and column2 from table2 based on a condition, and the result of the subquery is used as input for an INSERT statement to insert rows into table1.

optimising Subqueries for Performance

Subqueries can have an impact on query performance, especially when dealing with large tables or complex queries. Here are some tips for optimising subqueries for better performance:

1. Use appropriate indexes: Just like with regular queries, indexes can greatly improve the performance of subqueries. Make sure that the columns used in the subquery's WHERE clause or JOIN conditions are indexed for faster retrieval of data.
2. Limit the use of correlated subqueries: Correlated subqueries can be less efficient compared to non-correlated subqueries, as they can result in multiple queries being executed for each row in the outer query. Try to minimize the use of correlated subqueries and use other techniques, such as JOINs or temporary tables, when possible.
3. Use EXISTS or NOT EXISTS instead of COUNT or MAX: When checking for the existence or non-existence of rows in a subquery, using EXISTS or NOT EXISTS

operators can be more efficient compared to using COUNT or MAX functions. EXISTS and NOT EXISTS only need to determine if any rows exist or do not exist, respectively, in the subquery, whereas COUNT or MAX functions need to calculate the aggregate value for all rows in the subquery.

4. Be mindful of subquery depth: Avoid excessive nesting of subqueries, as it can make the query harder to read and maintain, and can also degrade query performance. Limit the depth of subqueries to keep the query structure simple and easy to understand.

5. Use appropriate join types: When using subqueries in the FROM or JOIN clauses, be mindful of the join types used. INNER JOINs are generally more efficient compared to OUTER JOINs, as they retrieve only the matching rows from both tables. Choose the appropriate join type based on the requirements of your query to optimize performance.

Conclusion

Subqueries are a powerful tool in SQL Server that allow you to perform complex operations, retrieve related data, and perform calculations based on the values of the main query. They can be used in various clauses of a query, such as WHERE, FROM, and SELECT, and can be combined with other SQL features to achieve advanced functionality. However, it's important to use subqueries judiciously and optimize them for performance to ensure efficient query execution, especially when dealing with large tables or complex queries.

In this chapter, we covered the basics of creating and using subqueries in SQL Server, including the syntax, types of subqueries, and examples of how to use them in different scenarios. We also discussed advanced subquery techniques, such as subqueries with EXISTS and NOT EXISTS, IN and NOT IN operators, correlated subqueries, and using subqueries in INSERT, UPDATE, and DELETE statements. Lastly, we provided some tips for optimising subqueries for better performance.

With a solid understanding of subqueries and their various techniques, software developers can leverage their capabilities to write efficient and effective SQL Server queries that meet the needs of their applications. Subqueries are a valuable tool in the SQL Server developer's toolbox, and mastering their usage can greatly enhance the ability to retrieve, manipulate, and analyze data in a relational database system.

Chapter - 3.3 - Using Built-in Functions to Manipulate Data

As a software developer, working with SQL Server is an essential skill for building robust and scalable applications. SQL Server provides a wide range of built-in functions that allow you to manipulate data in your databases efficiently. These functions are powerful tools that can be used to perform various operations on data, such as performing calculations, formatting values, extracting information, and more. In this chapter, we will explore the different types of built-in functions in SQL Server and how they can be used to manipulate data effectively.

Introduction to Built-in Functions

Built-in functions in SQL Server are predefined functions that are available for use in SQL queries. They are grouped into various categories based on their functionality, such as string functions, numeric functions, date and time functions, and more. These functions can be used in SQL queries to perform operations on columns, literals, or expressions, and they can also be used in conjunction with other SQL clauses, such as SELECT, WHERE, GROUP BY, and ORDER BY, to manipulate data.

SQL Server provides a wide range of built-in functions that cater to different data manipulation needs. Some of the common categories of built-in functions in SQL Server are:

- String Functions: These functions are used to manipulate string values, such as concatenating strings, extracting substrings, converting case, and more. Examples of string functions in SQL Server include CONCAT, SUBSTRING, UPPER, LOWER, and REPLACE.
- Numeric Functions: These functions are used to perform calculations on numeric values, such as arithmetic operations, rounding, and more. Examples of numeric functions in SQL Server include SUM, AVG, ROUND, and ABS.
- Date and Time Functions: These functions are used to work with date and time values, such as calculating date differences, extracting parts of dates, formatting dates, and more. Examples of date and time functions in SQL Server include GETDATE, DATEADD, DATEDIFF, and FORMAT.
- Conversion Functions: These functions are used to convert data types from one type to another, such as converting strings to numbers, dates to strings, and more. Examples of conversion functions in SQL Server include CAST, CONVERT, and TRY_CONVERT.
- Aggregate Functions: These functions are used to perform calculations on sets of values and return a single value as the result, such as calculating the average, sum, or count of a set of values. Examples of aggregate functions in SQL Server include COUNT, SUM, AVG, MAX, and MIN.

- Logical Functions: These functions are used to perform logical operations, such as evaluating conditions and returning boolean values. Examples of logical functions in SQL Server include CASE, NULLIF, and COALESCE.
- System Functions: These functions provide information about the SQL Server system, such as retrieving server information, getting current user information, and more. Examples of system functions in SQL Server include @@SERVERNAME, CURRENT_USER, and HOST_NAME.

Using String Functions

String functions are commonly used in SQL Server to manipulate string values, such as concatenating strings, extracting substrings, and changing the case of strings. Let's look at some examples of string functions and how they can be used to manipulate data.

CONCAT:

The CONCAT function is used to concatenate two or more strings together. It takes multiple string values as input and returns a single concatenated string. For example, the following query concatenates the first name and last name columns of a table to create a full name:

```sql
SELECT CONCAT(first_name, ' ', last_name) AS full_name
FROM employees;
```

SUBSTRING:

The SUBSTRING function is used to extract a substring from a string value. It takes three arguments: the input string, the starting position of the substring, and the length of the substring. For example, the following query extracts the first 3 characters from the 'product_name' column of a 'products' table:

```sql
SELECT SUBSTRING(product_name, 1, 3) AS short_name
FROM products;
```

UPPER and LOWER:

The UPPER and LOWER functions are used to convert the case of string values. UPPER converts a string to uppercase, while LOWER converts a string to lowercase.

For example, the following query converts the 'city' column of a 'customers' table to uppercase:

```
SELECT UPPER(city) AS city_upper
FROM customers;
```

REPLACE:

The REPLACE function is used to replace occurrences of a substring within a string with a new substring. It takes three arguments: the input string, the substring to be replaced, and the new substring.

For example, the following query replaces all occurrences of 'Mr.' with 'Ms.' in the 'title' column of an 'employees' table:

```
SELECT REPLACE(title, 'Mr.', 'Ms.') AS updated_title
FROM employees;
```

LEN:

The LEN function is used to calculate the length of a string. It takes a string value as input and returns the number of characters in the string. For example, the following query calculates the length of the 'product_description' column of a 'products' table:

```
SELECT LEN(product_description) AS description_length
FROM products;
```

These are just a few examples of the string functions available in SQL Server. String functions can be combined with other SQL clauses, such as WHERE, GROUP BY, and ORDER BY, to perform more complex string manipulations as per your requirements.

Using Numeric Functions

Numeric functions in SQL Server are used to perform calculations on numeric values, such as arithmetic operations, rounding, and more. Let's explore some examples of numeric functions and how they can be used to manipulate data.

SUM:

The SUM function is used to calculate the sum of a set of numeric values. It takes a column or an expression as input and returns the total sum of the values. For example, the following query calculates the total revenue from the 'sales' table:

```sql
SELECT SUM(revenue) AS total_revenue
FROM sales;
```

AVG:

The AVG function is used to calculate the average of a set of numeric values. It takes a column or an expression as input and returns the average of the values. For example, the following query calculates the average salary of employees in a 'employees' table:

```sql
SELECT AVG(salary) AS average_salary
FROM employees;
```

ROUND:

The ROUND function is used to round a numeric value to a specified number of decimal places. It takes two arguments: the numeric value and the number of decimal places to round to. For example, the following query rounds the 'price' column of a 'products' table to two decimal places:

```sql
SELECT ROUND(price, 2) AS rounded_price
FROM products;
```

ABS:

The ABS function is used to return the absolute value of a numeric value. It takes a numeric value as input and returns its absolute value. For example, the following query calculates the absolute difference between two numeric columns in a 'sales' table:

```sql
SELECT ABS(quantity_sold - quantity_returned) AS absolute_difference
FROM sales;
```

RAND:

The RAND function is used to generate a random float value between 0 and 1. It can be used to generate random values for testing or sampling purposes. For example, the following query generates a random discount value between 0 and 0.5 for a 'products' table:

```sql
SELECT product_name, price, price * RAND() * 0.5 AS discount
FROM products;
```

These are just a few examples of the numeric functions available in SQL Server. Numeric functions can be used in various scenarios to perform calculations, aggregations, and data transformations as needed in your database.

Date and Time Functions

Date and time functions in SQL Server are used to work with date and time values, such as extracting parts of a date or time, formatting date and time values, and performing date and time calculations. Let's explore some examples of date and time functions and how they can be used to manipulate data.

GETDATE:

The GETDATE function is used to get the current date and time in the SQL Server system's time zone. It does not take any arguments and returns the current date and time as a datetime value. For example, the following query retrieves the current date and time:

```sql
SELECT GETDATE() AS current_datetime;
```

DATEPART:

The DATEPART function is used to extract a specific part of a date or time value, such as the year, month, day, hour, minute, or second. It takes two arguments: the date or time value and the part to be extracted. For example, the following query extracts the year and month from a 'sales' table:

```sql
SELECT DATEPART(year, order_date) AS order_year, DATEPART(month,
order_date) AS order_month
FROM sales;
```

DATEADD:

The DATEADD function is used to perform date arithmetic in SQL Server. It is used to add or subtract a specified value (such as days, months, or years) to a date or time value. It takes three arguments: the part to be added or subtracted, the value to be added or subtracted, and the date or time value. For example, the following query adds 7 days to the 'order_date' column of a 'sales' table:

```sql
SELECT DATEADD(day, 7, order_date) AS new_order_date
FROM sales;
```

CONVERT:

The CONVERT function is used to convert date and time values from one data type to another in SQL Server. It takes two arguments: the data type to which the value should be converted and the value to be converted. For example, the following query converts the 'order_date' column of a 'sales' table to a date string in the format 'dd/MM/yyyy':

```sql
SELECT CONVERT(varchar(10), order_date, 103) AS order_date_string
FROM sales;
```

DATEDIFF:

The DATEDIFF function is used to calculate the difference between two date or time values in SQL Server. It takes three arguments: the part for which the difference should be calculated, the start date, and the end date. For example, the following query calculates the number of days between the 'order_date' and 'ship_date' columns of a 'orders' table:

```sql
SELECT DATEDIFF(day, order_date, ship_date) AS days_to_ship
FROM orders;
```

These are just a few examples of the date and time functions available in SQL Server. Date and time functions can be used to perform various date and time-related calculations and manipulations, such as extracting date parts, performing date arithmetic, and formatting date and time values according to your requirements.

Type Conversion Functions

Type conversion functions in SQL Server are used to convert data from one data type to another. They are useful when you need to perform operations or comparisons between different data types. Let's explore some examples of type conversion functions and how they can be used to manipulate data.

CAST:

The CAST function is used to explicitly convert a value from one data type to another. It takes two arguments: the value to be converted and the data type to which the value should be converted. For example, the following query converts an integer column 'age' to a decimal data type with two decimal places:

```sql
SELECT CAST(age AS decimal(10,2)) AS age_decimal
FROM users;
```

CONVERT:

The CONVERT function, which we have already discussed in the date and time functions section, can also be used for type conversion. It can be used to convert data from one data type to another, including date and time values, strings, and numeric values. For example, the following query converts a datetime column 'created_at' to a string in the format 'yyyy-MM-dd HH:mm:ss':

```sql
SELECT CONVERT(varchar(19), created_at, 120) AS created_at_string
FROM orders;
```

TRY_CAST and TRY_CONVERT:

The TRY_CAST and TRY_CONVERT functions are similar to the CAST and CONVERT functions, respectively, with one key difference: they do not throw an error if the conversion fails. Instead, they return a NULL value. This can be useful when you want to handle potential conversion errors gracefully. For example, the following query uses TRY_CAST to convert a string column 'salary' to a numeric data type, and returns NULL for invalid values:

```sql
SELECT TRY_CAST(salary AS decimal(10,2)) AS salary_decimal
FROM employees;
```

PARSE:

The PARSE function is used to convert a string to a specified data type in SQL Server. It takes two arguments: the string to be converted, and the data type to which the string should be converted. For example, the following query converts a string column 'amount' to a money data type:

```sql
SELECT PARSE(amount AS money) AS amount_money
FROM transactions;
```

These are some of the type conversion functions available in SQL Server. Type conversion functions can be used to convert data from one data type to another, allowing you to perform operations or comparisons on different data types as needed in your database.

String Functions

String functions in SQL Server are used to manipulate and process strings, which are a common data type used for representing text or character data. String functions can be used to perform tasks such as concatenation, substitution, trimming, and formatting of string values. Let's explore some examples of string functions and how they can be used to manipulate data.

CONCAT:

The CONCAT function is used to concatenate two or more strings into a single string in SQL Server. It takes two or more arguments, which are the strings to be concatenated. For example, the following query concatenates the 'first_name' and 'last_name' columns of a 'users' table:

```sql
SELECT CONCAT(first_name, ' ', last_name) AS full_name
FROM users;
```

LEN:

The LEN function is used to calculate the length of a string in SQL Server. It takes a single argument, which is the string whose length needs to be calculated. For example, the following query calculates the length of the 'product_name' column of a 'products' table:

```
SELECT LEN(product_name) AS product_name_length
FROM products;
```

LEFT and RIGHT:

The LEFT and RIGHT functions are used to extract a specified number of characters from the left or right side of a string in SQL Server, respectively. They take two arguments: the string from which characters need to be extracted, and the number of characters to be extracted. For example, the following query extracts the first three characters from the 'city' column of a 'customers' table:

```
SELECT LEFT(city, 3) AS city_prefix
FROM customers;
```

REPLACE:

The REPLACE function is used to replace all occurrences of a specified substring with another substring in a string in SQL Server. It takes three arguments: the original string, the substring to be replaced, and the substring to replace it with. For example, the following query replaces all occurrences of the word 'old' with 'new' in the 'description' column of a 'products' table:

```
SELECT REPLACE(description, 'old', 'new') AS updated_description
FROM products;
```

CHARINDEX:

The CHARINDEX function is used to find the starting position of a substring within a string in SQL Server. It takes two arguments: the substring to be searched, and the string within which the substring needs to be found. For example, the following query finds the position of the substring 'SQL' in the 'title' column of a 'books' table:

```
SELECT CHARINDEX('SQL', title) AS substring_position
FROM books;
```

LOWER and UPPER:

The LOWER and UPPER functions are used to convert a string to lowercase and uppercase, respectively, in SQL Server. They take a single argument, which is the string to be converted. For example, the following query converts the 'last_name' column of a 'users' table to uppercase:

```
SELECT UPPER(last_name) AS last_name_upper
FROM users;
```

LTRIM and RTRIM:

The LTRIM and RTRIM functions are used to remove leading and trailing spaces, respectively, from a string in SQL Server. They take a single argument, which is the string from which spaces need to be trimmed. For example, the following query removes leading and trailing spaces from the 'address' column of a 'customers' table:

```
SELECT LTRIM(RTRIM(address)) AS trimmed_address
FROM customers;
```

SUBSTRING:

The SUBSTRING function is used to extract a portion of a string in SQL Server. It takes three arguments: the string from which characters need to be extracted, the starting position of the extraction, and the number of characters to be extracted. For example, the following query extracts the first five characters from the 'description' column of a 'products' table:

```
SELECT SUBSTRING(description, 1, 5) AS product_prefix
FROM products;
```

These are some of the commonly used string functions in SQL Server. String functions can be used to manipulate and process string data to perform various tasks such as concatenation, substitution, trimming, and formatting.

Aggregate Functions

Aggregate functions in SQL Server are used to perform calculations on sets of values and return a single result. They are often used in conjunction with the GROUP BY clause to perform calculations on groups of rows. Aggregate functions are used to perform operations such as counting, summing, averaging, finding the maximum or minimum value, and more. Let's explore some examples of aggregate functions and how they can be used to manipulate data.

COUNT:

The COUNT function is used to count the number of non-null values in a column or a set of values in SQL Server. It takes a single argument, which is the column or set of values to be counted. For example, the following query counts the number of orders in an 'orders' table:

```sql
SELECT COUNT(*) AS order_count
FROM orders;
```

SUM:

The SUM function is used to calculate the sum of values in a column or a set of values in SQL Server. It takes a single argument, which is the column or set of values to be summed. For example, the following query calculates the total sales amount in a 'sales' table:

```sql
SELECT SUM(sales_amount) AS total_sales
FROM sales;
```

AVG:

The AVG function is used to calculate the average of values in a column or a set of values in SQL Server. It takes a single argument, which is the column or set of values to be averaged. For example, the following query calculates the average salary of employees in an 'employees' table:

```sql
SELECT AVG(salary) AS average_salary
FROM employees;
```

MIN and MAX:

The MIN and MAX functions are used to find the minimum and maximum values in a column or a set of values in SQL Server, respectively. They take a single argument, which is the column or set of values to be evaluated. For example, the following query finds the minimum and maximum prices of products in a 'products' table:

```sql
SELECT MIN(price) AS min_price, MAX(price) AS max_price
FROM products;
```

GROUP BY:

The GROUP BY clause is used in conjunction with aggregate functions to group rows based on one or more columns and perform calculations on each group separately in SQL Server. For example, the following query groups orders by customer ID and calculates the total order amount for each customer:

```sql
SELECT customer_id, SUM(order_amount) AS total_order_amount
FROM orders
GROUP BY customer_id;
```

HAVING:

The HAVING clause is used in conjunction with the GROUP BY clause to filter the groups of rows that are generated by the GROUP BY clause based on a condition in SQL Server. For example, the following query groups orders by customer ID and calculates the total order amount for each customer, but only includes customers whose total order amount is greater than $1000:

```sql
SELECT customer_id, SUM(order_amount) AS total_order_amount
FROM orders
GROUP BY customer_id
HAVING SUM(order_amount) > 1000;
```

Aggregate functions and the GROUP BY clause are powerful tools for manipulating data in SQL Server. They allow developers to perform calculations on sets of values, group data based on specific criteria, and filter groups of rows based on conditions.

Conclusion

Built-in functions are an essential component of SQL Server and provide developers with a wide range of tools to manipulate data. In this chapter, we explored some of the most commonly used built-in functions in SQL Server, including string, numeric, and date and time functions. We also discussed how aggregate functions and the GROUP BY clause can be used to perform calculations on sets of values, group data based on specific criteria, and filter groups of rows based on conditions. By mastering built-in functions in SQL Server, developers can become more efficient and productive in their data manipulation tasks.

They can easily perform various data transformations, calculations, and formatting operations on data within the SQL Server database itself, without the need for additional code or processing outside the database.

As a software developer, it is crucial to have a solid understanding of these built-in functions in SQL Server, as they can greatly enhance your ability to manipulate data efficiently and effectively. By leveraging the power of these functions, you can streamline your database operations and achieve better performance and accuracy in your applications.

In the next chapter, we will dive deeper into advanced topics related to SQL Server, including working with views, stored procedures, and triggers, as well as optimising database performance and security. These topics will provide you with a comprehensive understanding of SQL Server and its advanced features, enabling you to build robust, scalable, and secure applications. Stay tuned for the next chapter and continue your journey to becoming a SQL Server expert!

Chapter 3.4 - Using SQL Agent in SQL Server

Introduction

As a software developer working with SQL Server, you may find yourself needing to perform tasks on a regular basis, such as executing stored procedures or performing backups. This is where SQL Agent comes in. SQL Agent is a component of SQL Server that allows you to automate tasks and schedule them to run at specific times. In this chapter, we will explore the basics of SQL Agent and how you can use it to automate tasks in SQL Server.

What is SQL Agent?

SQL Agent is a component of SQL Server that provides a framework for executing tasks on a schedule. It is a Windows service that is installed with SQL Server and runs in the background. SQL Agent is used to automate tasks, such as executing SQL Server Integration Services (SSIS) packages, running stored procedures, and performing backups.

SQL Agent is a powerful tool that can help you manage and maintain your SQL Server environment. With SQL Agent, you can create jobs, which are sets of one or more steps that perform a specific task. You can schedule these jobs to run at specific times or in response to specific events. You can also configure SQL Agent to notify you when a job completes or if there is an error.

Creating a SQL Agent Job

To create a SQL Agent job, you need to have SQL Server Management Studio (SSMS) installed on your computer. SSMS is a graphical user interface that allows you to manage and administer SQL Server. Once you have SSMS installed, you can create a new job by following these steps:

Open SSMS and connect to the SQL Server instance where you want to create the job.
In Object Explorer, expand the SQL Server Agent node.
Right-click on the Jobs folder and select New Job from the context menu.
In the New Job dialog box, enter a name for the job and a description (optional).
In the Steps section, click New to create a new step.
In the New Job Step dialog box, enter a name for the step and select the type of command you want to execute (SQL Server Integration Services package, T-SQL script, or CmdExec command).
Enter the command or script that you want to execute in the Command box.
Configure any additional settings, such as logging options or notifications.

Click OK to save the step and return to the New Job dialog box.
Configure any additional settings, such as the schedule or alerts.
Click OK to save the job.
Once you have created a job, you can view and manage it in SSMS. You can start, stop, or modify the job as needed.

Scheduling a SQL Agent Job

One of the most powerful features of SQL Agent is the ability to schedule jobs to run at specific times or in response to specific events. To schedule a job, you need to create a schedule object in SQL Server Agent. A schedule defines when a job runs and how often it runs.

To create a new schedule, follow these steps:

In SSMS, expand the SQL Server Agent node.
Right-click on the Schedules folder and select New Schedule from the context menu.
In the New Job Schedule dialog box, enter a name for the schedule and a description (optional).
Specify the frequency of the schedule (once, daily, weekly, or monthly).
Configure the schedule details, such as the start time and end time, and the days of the week on which the job should run.
Click OK to save the schedule.
Once you have created a schedule, you can assign it to a job. To assign a schedule to a job, follow these steps:

Open the job in SSMS.
Click on the Steps section.
3. Click on the Schedule button to open the Schedule Properties dialog box.

Select the schedule that you want to use for the job.
Click OK to save the schedule and return to the New Job dialog box.
Click OK to save the job.
Now the job will run on the schedule that you have defined.

Viewing Job History and Alerts

SQL Agent also provides tools for monitoring job history and alerts. Job history allows you to view information about the execution of a job, including the start time, end time, and any errors or warnings that occurred. To view job history, follow these steps:

In SSMS, expand the SQL Server Agent node.
Expand the Jobs folder and select the job that you want to view.
Right-click on the job and select View History from the context menu.
In the Job History window, you can view information about the job runs.
You can also configure SQL Agent to send alerts when certain events occur, such as a job failure or a low disk space condition. To configure alerts, follow these steps:

In SSMS, expand the SQL Server Agent node.
Right-click on the Alerts folder and select New Alert from the context menu.
In the New Alert dialog box, enter a name for the alert and a description (optional).
Select the type of alert that you want to configure (SQL Server error, SQL Server performance condition, or Windows event log).
Configure the alert settings, such as the error number or severity level, or the performance counter threshold.
Select the actions that you want to take when the alert is triggered, such as sending an email notification or running a job.
Click OK to save the alert.
Now when the alert conditions are met, SQL Agent will take the configured actions.

Conclusion

SQL Agent is a powerful tool that allows you to automate tasks and manage your SQL Server environment. By creating jobs and schedules, you can automate routine tasks and ensure that they are performed consistently and reliably. You can also use job history and alerts to monitor the performance of your SQL Server and quickly respond to any issues that arise. With SQL Agent, you can save time and improve the efficiency of your SQL Server environment.

Best Practices for Using SQL Agent

To ensure that SQL Agent operates efficiently and effectively, there are a number of best practices that you should follow:

Use a separate service account for SQL Agent: By using a separate service account for SQL Agent, you can improve security and ensure that the agent has the necessary permissions to perform its tasks.

Monitor job duration: If a job takes longer than expected to complete, it can impact the performance of other jobs and SQL Server operations. Be sure to monitor job duration and adjust job schedules and settings as needed to ensure that jobs complete in a timely manner.

Use appropriate schedules: When creating schedules for jobs, be sure to use schedules that align with the requirements of the job. For example, if a job needs to run every hour, use an hourly schedule rather than a daily schedule.

Use appropriate notification settings: When configuring job notifications, be sure to use appropriate notification settings based on the severity of the job. For example, you may want to configure email notifications for critical jobs, but only log notifications for less important jobs.

Monitor job history and alerts: Be sure to regularly monitor job history and alerts to identify issues and respond quickly to any problems that arise.

Regularly maintain SQL Agent: Regularly performing maintenance tasks such as updating SQL Agent and applying security patches can help to ensure that the agent operates effectively and efficiently.

By following these best practices, you can ensure that SQL Agent operates effectively and efficiently and helps to improve the performance and reliability of your SQL Server environment.

Conclusion

SQL Agent is a powerful tool that allows you to automate tasks and manage your SQL Server environment. By using SQL Agent to create jobs and schedules, you can automate routine tasks and ensure that they are performed consistently and reliably. Additionally, by monitoring job history and alerts, you can quickly identify and respond to any issues that arise. By following best practices for using SQL Agent, you can ensure that it operates efficiently and effectively and helps to improve the performance and reliability of your SQL Server environment.

Troubleshooting SQL Agent

Even with the best practices in place, issues with SQL Agent may still arise. Some common issues include jobs not running as scheduled, jobs running slowly, or errors occurring during job execution. Here are some troubleshooting steps that you can take to address these issues:

Verify that SQL Agent is running: If SQL Agent is not running, no jobs will be executed. Check the SQL Server Configuration Manager to ensure that SQL Agent is running.

Check job schedules: If a job is not running as expected, check the job schedule to ensure that it is configured correctly.

Check job steps: If a job is running slowly or encountering errors, check the job steps to ensure that they are correct and optimised.

Check job history: If a job is encountering errors or running slowly, check the job history to identify any issues or errors that occurred during the job run.

Check SQL Server logs: If SQL Agent encounters an error, it may be logged in the SQL Server logs. Check the logs for errors related to SQL Agent.

Check system resources: If SQL Agent is running slowly, check the system resources such as CPU and memory usage to ensure that there are no resource constraints.

By following these troubleshooting steps, you can identify and address issues with SQL Agent and ensure that it operates effectively and efficiently.

Conclusion

SQL Agent is a powerful tool that allows you to automate tasks and manage your SQL Server environment. By using SQL Agent to create jobs and schedules, you can automate routine tasks and ensure that they are performed consistently and reliably. Additionally, by monitoring job history and alerts, you can quickly identify and respond to any issues that arise. By following best practices for using SQL Agent and troubleshooting issues as they arise, you can ensure that it operates efficiently and effectively and helps to improve the performance and reliability of your SQL Server environment.

Advanced Features of SQL Agent

In addition to creating jobs and schedules, SQL Agent offers a number of advanced features that can help you to further customize and optimise your SQL Server environment. Here are a few examples:

Multi-server jobs: With multi-server jobs, you can create jobs that run on multiple instances of SQL Server. This can be useful for managing large environments with multiple instances.

Proxy accounts: Proxy accounts allow you to specify a different account to run a job step. This can be useful for granting limited permissions to job steps while maintaining security.

PowerShell integration: SQL Agent includes integration with PowerShell, allowing you to run PowerSh Conclusion ell scripts as job steps. This can be useful for automating complex tasks or integrating with other systems.

Alerts: SQL Agent includes a powerful alerting system that allows you to configure alerts based on job status, SQL Server errors, and more. Alerts can be configured to send email notifications, write to the Windows Event Log, or execute a job step.

By leveraging these advanced features of SQL Agent, you can further customize and optimise your SQL Server environment to meet the needs of your organization.

SQL Agent is a powerful tool that allows you to automate tasks and manage your SQL Server environment. By using SQL Agent to create jobs and schedules, you can automate routine tasks and ensure that they are performed consistently and reliably. Additionally, by monitoring job history and alerts, you can quickly identify and respond to any issues that arise. By following best practices for using SQL Agent, troubleshooting issues, and leveraging advanced features, you can ensure that it operates efficiently and effectively and helps to improve the performance and reliability of your SQL Server environment.

Conclusion

SQL Agent is an essential tool for software developers working with SQL Server. With SQL Agent, you can automate routine tasks, manage job schedules, and monitor job history and alerts. By following best practices for using SQL Agent, you can ensure that it operates efficiently and effectively, improving the performance and reliability of your SQL Server environment.

When troubleshooting issues with SQL Agent, there are several steps that you can take to identify and address issues quickly. By verifying that SQL Agent is running, checking job schedules and steps, reviewing job history, checking SQL Server logs, and monitoring system resources, you can quickly identify and address issues as they arise.

SQL Agent also includes several advanced features, such as multi-server jobs, proxy accounts, PowerShell integration, and alerts. By leveraging these features, you can further customize and optimise your SQL Server environment to meet the needs of your organization.

In conclusion, SQL Agent is a powerful tool that can help you automate routine tasks and manage your SQL Server environment. By following best practices, troubleshooting issues as they arise, and leveraging advanced features, you can ensure that SQL Agent operates efficiently and effectively, improving the performance and reliability of your SQL Server environment.

Chapter 3.5 - Storing and managing stored procedures

In the world of software development, efficiency, maintainability, and security are of utmost importance. As a software developer working with SQL Server, one powerful tool that can significantly enhance all these aspects is a Stored Procedure. Stored procedures are a fundamental feature of SQL Server that allow you to encapsulate and execute a series of SQL statements as a single unit of work. They not only promote code reusability but also help optimize database performance and enhance security. In this chapter, we will delve deep into the world of stored procedures, understanding their significance, syntax, and best practices for leveraging their full potential in your applications.

Introduction to Stored Procedures

A stored procedure is a precompiled set of SQL statements stored in the database server. It acts as a reusable, modular, and self-contained unit that can be executed with a single call. The concept of stored procedures was introduced to enhance the efficiency of database operations and simplify application development. By encapsulating complex or frequently used SQL logic in stored procedures, you can avoid code duplication, promote consistency, and reduce network traffic.

Benefits of Using Stored Procedures

Stored procedures offer numerous benefits that can significantly impact the development process and the overall performance of your applications:

Code Reusability:

Stored procedures can be reused across multiple applications or different parts of the same application, leading to a more modular and maintainable codebase.

Performance Optimization:

Stored procedures are precompiled, which means they are executed faster than dynamic SQL queries, improving overall database performance.

Security Enhancement:

By using stored procedures, you can grant users permission to execute the procedure without granting direct access to underlying tables, reducing the risk of unauthorised data access.

Centralised Business Logic:

Complex business logic can be encapsulated within stored procedures, ensuring consistency in data manipulation and reducing the chances of bugs due to inconsistent logic.

Reduced Network Traffic:

Calling a stored procedure from your application involves transmitting only the procedure name and parameters, minimizing the data transfer between the database server and the application.

Version Control:

Since stored procedures are stored in the database, version control can be managed easily, ensuring that the correct version is being used across all applications.

Creating Stored Procedures

To create a stored procedure in SQL Server, you use the CREATE PROCEDURE statement followed by the procedure's name and the SQL statements enclosed within a BEGIN...END block. The basic syntax for creating a stored procedure is as follows:

```
CREATE PROCEDURE procedure_name
    -- Parameter declarations (optional)
    @parameter_name data_type [ = default_value ],
    -- Additional parameters (optional)
    @parameter_name data_type [ = default_value ]
AS
BEGIN
    -- SQL statements for the procedure
END;
```

In this syntax:

procedure_name: The name of the stored procedure you want to create. It must be unique within the schema.

@parameter_name: The name of the input parameter for the procedure. Parameters allow you to pass values to the procedure.

data_type: The data type of the parameter. It can be any valid SQL Server data type.

[= default_value]: An optional default value for the parameter. If a default value is specified, the parameter becomes optional.

Creating Simple Stored Procedures

Let's start by creating a simple stored procedure that retrieves all employees from an 'employees' table:

```sql
CREATE PROCEDURE GetEmployees
AS
BEGIN
    SELECT * FROM employees;
END;
```

In this example, we are creating a stored procedure named 'GetEmployees' that fetches all records from the 'employees' table.

Stored Procedures with Input Parameters

Stored procedures can accept input parameters, which allow you to pass values to the procedure for filtering or processing data. Let's create a stored procedure that retrieves employees based on their department:

```sql
CREATE PROCEDURE GetEmployeesByDepartment
    @dept_name NVARCHAR(50)
AS
BEGIN
    SELECT * FROM employees WHERE department = @dept_name;
END;
```

In this example, we are creating a stored procedure named 'GetEmployeesByDepartment' with a single input parameter @dept_name. The procedure selects all employees from the 'employees' table where the 'department' column matches the provided department name.

Stored Procedures with Output Parameters

Stored procedures can also have output parameters, which allow you to return values back to the calling code. Let's create a stored procedure that calculates the total salary for a department and returns it through an output parameter:

```sql
CREATE PROCEDURE CalculateTotalSalary
    @dept_name NVARCHAR(50),
    @total_salary DECIMAL(10, 2) OUTPUT
AS
BEGIN
    SELECT @total_salary = SUM(salary) FROM employees WHERE department =
@dept_name;
END;
```

In this example, we are creating a stored procedure named 'CalculateTotalSalary' with two parameters: @dept_name as an input parameter and @total_salary as an output parameter. The procedure calculates the total salary for the provided department and stores the result in the output parameter @total_salary.

Executing Stored Procedures

Once you have created a stored procedure, you can execute it using the EXECUTE or EXEC keyword, followed by the procedure name and any input parameters if required. Let's see how to execute the 'GetEmployees' and 'GetEmployeesByDepartment' stored procedures we created earlier:

```
-- Executing the 'GetEmployees' stored procedure
EXEC GetEmployees;

-- Executing the 'GetEmployeesByDepartment' stored procedure with the
department parameter
EXEC GetEmployeesByDepartment @dept_name = 'Sales';
```

You can execute the 'CalculateTotalSalary' stored procedure that we created with an output parameter as follows:

```
DECLARE @total_salary DECIMAL(10, 2);

EXEC CalculateTotalSalary @dept_name = 'Finance', @total_salary =
@total_salary OUTPUT;

PRINT 'Total salary for Finance department: ' + CAST(@total_salary AS
NVARCHAR(50));
```

In this example, we declare a variable @total_salary to hold the output value from the procedure and pass it to the stored procedure as an output parameter.

Modifying and Dropping Stored Procedures

As your application evolves, you may need to modify or update existing stored procedures. To modify a stored procedure, you can use the ALTER PROCEDURE statement, followed by the updated procedure definition. Note that modifying a stored procedure does not affect the permissions granted to it.

```sql
ALTER PROCEDURE GetEmployees
AS
BEGIN
    SELECT employee_id, first_name, last_name, hire_date
    FROM employees
    ORDER BY hire_date DESC;
END;
```

In this example, we modify the 'GetEmployees' stored procedure to retrieve only specific columns from the 'employees' table and sort the results based on the 'hire_date' in descending order.

If a stored procedure is no longer needed or needs to be replaced, you can drop it from the database using the DROP PROCEDURE statement:

```sql
DROP PROCEDURE GetEmployees;
```

Please exercise caution when dropping stored procedures, as it can permanently remove the procedure and its associated permissions.

Best Practices for Stored Procedures

To make the most of stored procedures and ensure optimal performance and security, it is essential to follow some best practices when creating and using them:

Parameterize Queries

Always parameterize your stored procedures to prevent SQL injection attacks and improve performance. Avoid concatenating input values directly into SQL statements. Instead, pass them as parameters to the stored procedure.

Use Appropriate Data Types

Choose the appropriate data types for input and output parameters in your stored procedures. Using data types that match the underlying table columns can improve performance and avoid unnecessary data conversions.

Handle Errors Gracefully

Implement error handling within your stored procedures to capture and handle exceptions. You can use the TRY...CATCH construct to catch errors and gracefully handle them, providing meaningful error messages to the calling code.

Limit the Number of Rows Returned

Avoid returning a large number of rows from your stored procedures. If the result set is too large, it can impact performance and lead to excessive network traffic. Consider using pagination techniques or filtering data within the stored procedure.

Consider Using Temp Tables

In some cases, using temporary tables within a stored procedure can improve performance by reducing the need for complex joins or repetitive calculations. However, use temp tables judiciously, as they can also introduce additional overhead.

Use SET NOCOUNT ON

By default, SQL Server returns the number of rows affected by each SQL statement. In stored procedures, this can lead to additional network traffic. To suppress this message and improve performance, use the SET NOCOUNT ON statement at the beginning of the stored procedure.

```
CREATE PROCEDURE SampleProcedure
AS
BEGIN
    SET NOCOUNT ON;
    -- Rest of the stored procedure code
END;
```

Avoid Using SELECT *

Be specific with column selections in your stored procedures. Avoid using SELECT * to retrieve all columns from a table. Instead, explicitly list the required columns to reduce network traffic and improve maintainability.

Review Execution Plans

Periodically review the execution plans of your stored procedures using tools like SQL Server Management Studio or SQL Server Profiler. optimising query plans can significantly enhance performance.

Regularly Update Statistics

Keep your statistics up to date to ensure the query optimizer makes optimal choices when generating execution plans for your stored procedures. Outdated statistics can lead to suboptimal performance.

Document Your Stored Procedures

Document your stored procedures thoroughly, including their purpose, input parameters, output values, and any side effects. Proper documentation helps other developers understand the purpose and usage of stored procedures.

Conclusion

Stored procedures are a powerful tool that can greatly enhance the efficiency, maintainability, and security of your SQL Server applications. By encapsulating complex logic, promoting code reusability, and improving database performance, stored procedures play a crucial role in modern software development. In this chapter, we explored the benefits of using stored procedures, their syntax, and best practices for creating and using them effectively. As you continue your journey in SQL Server development, embrace the potential of stored procedures and leverage them to build robust, secure, and high-performance applications.

www.ingramcontent.com/pod-product-compliance
Lightning Source LLC
LaVergne TN
LVHW081802050326
832903LV00027B/2053